SILVER SPRING
AND THE
CIVIL WAR

Carolyn,
Hope you
enjoy this
as much as
I have!
Love, Janet

SILVER SPRING

AND THE

CIVIL WAR

ROBERT E. OSHEL, PHD

THE
History
PRESS

Published by The History Press
Charleston, SC 29403
www.historypress.net

Back cover, middle: Monument at Battleground National Cemetery honoring troops who lost their lives defending Washington in July 1864. *Photo by the author.*

First published 2014

Manufactured in the United States

ISBN 978.1.62619.417.5

Library of Congress CIP data applied for.

In times gone by I had passed over these roads little anticipating scenes like this, and a few years hence they will scarcely be believed to have occurred.

—Gideon Welles, Lincoln's secretary of the navy, July 12, 1864

CONTENTS

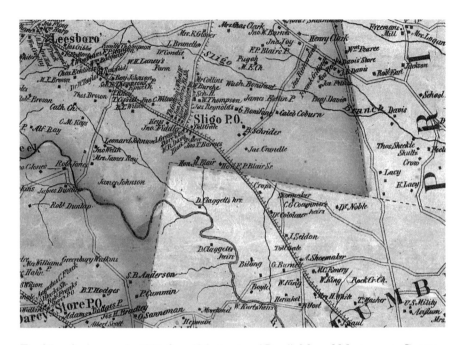

The Silver Spring area in 1865, from "Martenet and Bond's Map of Montgomery County, Maryland." "Sligo P.O." is today's downtown Silver Spring. The hashed road from "Leesboro" (Wheaton) past Sligo P.O. and into the District of Columbia is Georgia Avenue. Colesville Road runs from "Sligo P.O." to the top of the map, where it intersects with Forest Glen Road running to the left to its intersection with Georgia Avenue. Sligo Avenue runs to the right from Georgia Avenue just north of the District of Columbia to University Boulevard. "Sch[ool] H[ouse]" on Colesville Road is the site of City Place Mall. "Darcys Store P.O." at the lower left is Bethesda. *Library of Congress, Geography and Map Division.*

PREFACE

Silver Spring—the area in Montgomery County, Maryland, not just Francis Preston Blair's "Silver Spring"[1] estate—was the site of much of the action during the Confederates' 1864 invasion of the District of Columbia. Downtown Silver Spring and especially the Woodside and Woodside Park neighborhoods were in the thick of it, serving as the campsite for the main body of the Confederate army facing Washington. Homes, farm buildings and fields throughout the area were damaged by soldiers from both armies and by Union artillery shelling. Civil War relics, including unexploded ordnance, were found in the area well into the twentieth century. But Silver Spring was affected by the Civil War before General Jubal Early's famous 1864 attack and for years afterward. This book is the story of how the war affected Silver Spring and its residents. But since Silver Spring cannot be viewed in isolation, we tell a broader story as well.

Chapter 1

MONTGOMERY COUNTY AS CIVIL WAR LOOMS

Montgomery County in the 1850s was largely a rural area of farms owned by slaveholders. The population in 1860 was only 18,322, of whom almost 40 percent were black. Of the blacks, about 80 percent were slaves. Most slaveholders owned 10 or fewer slaves.[2]

As the country drifted toward the Civil War, the vast majority of local landowners in both Silver Spring and Montgomery County favored states' rights, and almost half of them favored secession if necessary to preserve slavery. This reflected the popular mood in Maryland.

In the 1860 election, Maryland voters strongly supported preserving slavery but only narrowly favored disbanding the Union if doing so was necessary to preserve slavery. The voters gave the state's eight electoral votes to Vice President John C. Breckinridge of the southern Democratic Party. The Democrats had split into northern and southern wings, each of which nominated its own candidates. Breckinridge, who was willing to dissolve the Union to preserve slavery, carried most of the states that ultimately seceded to form the Confederacy.

In Maryland, Breckinridge won a bare plurality of votes over John Bell of the Constitutional Union Party, which was largely composed of former Whigs and Know-Nothings. Bell favored compromise to preserve both the Union and slavery. Breckinridge won the Maryland electoral vote largely because of the size of his majority in Baltimore City. A Hagerstown newspaper commented that Breckinridge's victory "was accomplished by the naturalization of upwards of *Two Thousand* foreigners in Baltimore City

In this 1860 Louis Maurer cartoon for Currier and Ives titled *Storming the Castle*, Lincoln is shown preventing the other candidates from entering the White House, saying, "Ah! ha! Gentlemen! you need'nt think to catch me napping; for I am a regular Wide awake." At right, President Buchanan is trying to pull John C. Breckinridge through the window into the White House. Breckinridge says, "Ah, Mr. Buck! I am too weak to get up…and we shall be compelled to 'dissolve the Union.'" President Buchanan replies, "I'll do all I can to help you, Breck, but my strength is failing and I'm afraid you'll pull me out before I can pull you in." Meanwhile, in the center, John Bell frets at the corner, saying, "Hurry up Douglas! and get the door open, so I can get in, for the watchman is coming." Stephen A. Douglas replies, "Confound it! none of these Keys will unlock this door so I'd better be off, for old Abe is after me with a sharp stick." *Library of Congress.*

within four or five weeks of the election, all of whom, it is said, voted for Breckinridge."[3] "Baltimore gangs" and Maryland militia companies were also said to be strongly for secession.[4]

Outside Baltimore, most of the counties had a majority for Bell and preserving both slavery and the Union, but the results were close. In Montgomery County, Bell won with 1,155 votes, only 30 votes more than Breckinridge. Together, the two pro-slavery candidates had about 94 percent of the county's vote. Statewide, they took about 90 percent of the vote. But although Maryland voters were for preserving slavery, they almost unanimously rejected a ballot measure that would have enslaved Maryland's free blacks.[5]

Republican Abraham Lincoln finished a distant last in both Montgomery County and Maryland as a whole, trailing not only Bell and Breckinridge but also Stephen A. Douglas of the northern Democratic Party. Lincoln received only fifty votes (2 percent) in Montgomery County and only about 2.4 percent of the votes statewide.[6]

Sentiment in the Silver Spring area probably generally reflected the divided views of other county residents. However, the area did have two prominent residents who were Republicans: Francis Preston Blair and his son Montgomery Blair, who became Lincoln's postmaster general. Francis Preston Blair had come to Washington from Kentucky in 1830 to be editor of the *Globe* newspaper. He also was a member of Andrew Jackson's "kitchen cabinet" and continued to be politically prominent after Jackson's presidency ended. He was involved with the founding of the Republican Party.

Chapter 2

SILVER SPRING BEFORE THE WAR

In the 1860s, today's downtown Silver Spring was called Sligo. "Silver Spring," Francis Preston Blair's estate, was farther south near the District of Columbia boundary line. Sligo was a small settlement near where Colesville Road from the northeast ended at Georgia Avenue. An 1865 map shows Sligo had a total of eight structures, including a combined post office and store, two other stores and two blacksmith shops. There was also a tollgate on Georgia Avenue just south of the Colesville Road intersection. Another tollgate was on Colesville Road just north of today's Dale Drive (now site of Mrs. K's Tollhouse Restaurant). Sligo was so small that it probably would not have been on the map if it had not had a post office. Over the years, the Sligo name for the area gave way to Silver Spring. Both Sligo and the original "Silver Spring" were the location of action during the Civil War. So was the area north of Sligo.

The land immediately north of Sligo that was later developed as Woodside and Woodside Park consisted of two farms in the 1860s. Woodside and the west portion of Woodside Park were part of the Wilson farm, which straddled Georgia Avenue north of Colesville Road. The east portion of Woodside Park was the Burche farm. It was on the northwest side of Colesville Road east of the Wilson farm. Thomas Noble Wilson's home was on the northeast corner of the current Spring Street and Georgia Avenue intersection, where the southernmost row of Woodside Station town houses is now located. The exact location of Raymond W. Burche's home is unknown, but it was northwest of Colesville Road near today's Noyes and Mansion Drives.

Thomas Noble Wilson's home, shown here in 1952 shortly before its demolition but essentially unchanged since at least 1900. The dormer windows are believed to have been added after the Civil War. John C. Wilson inherited the home at his father's death. *Andrew Klink Collection.*

Francis Preston Blair's "Silver Spring" was clearly the showplace of the area. Blair had built his "Silver Spring" mansion as a summer home in 1842, but by the mid-1850s, he had left his home on Pennsylvania Avenue (today's presidential guest house, "Blair House") and lived at "Silver Spring" full time. "Silver Spring" was, more or less, on the southeast corner of Kennett and Newell Streets.

The estate was large. It was entered through the "Big Gate" off Georgia Avenue just inside Maryland. A drive wound through heavy woods and then through a row of horse chestnut trees and a row of silver pines to a

Francis Preston Blair of "Silver Spring." *Library of Congress.*

rustic bridge and the large home. The famous mica-flecked spring that gave the estate its name was some distance from the house at the end of a row of sugar maple trees flanked by landscaped lawns. There were also a rose garden, vegetable garden, grapery, peach orchard and fig bushes. Another feature was a large canebrake with plants brought from the ancestral home of Mrs. Blair, Canewood, in Kentucky.

The estate's dairy, stable and slave quarters were near the spring, as was the "Acorn" gazebo that still exists in Acorn Park off East-West Highway at 8060 Newell Street. Next to the Acorn was a large pond with "garlands of plants and roses on its banks in successive tiers, each tier of a kind to stand higher than its neighbor which was nearer the pond, so to the eye they rose from the water like seats in a colosseum [*sic*]."[7] Farther west were a mill powered by a water wheel and a large cattle barn. Even farther west was "Maria's bridge, a stucco spring stone ornamental structure." A mile-long path, which Francis Preston Blair called the "Grotto Walk," continued with periodic benches and garden bowers through the woods along a stream fed by the spring to the "Bishop's Chair"

Francis Preston Blair's "Silver Spring" is depicted in this 1995 mural by Mame Cohalan at Acorn Park's memory wall. *Photo by the author.*

grotto and then a rustic bridge composed of one huge, uneven stone. Beyond that were a series of grottoes and another spring. Other features were a large grotto "sunk deep into a hillside, above which grew lofty trees and underbrush," giving it "an air of mystery [suggesting] secrecy and seclusion"; "St. Andrew's Well"; "Violet Spring"; and a huge tree, "Hern's Oak." "The streams, and planting, gave the walk everywhere variety and beauty."[8]

Francis Preston Blair's family also had other mansions nearby. His son Montgomery Blair built "Falkland" about a third of a mile northwest of

"Silver Spring" on the family property, where the Blair Plaza shopping center is now located. In addition, "the Moorings" was built about three-eighths of a mile southeast of "Silver Spring" in 1850 for another son, James Blair, a naval officer—hence the mansion's name—who died in 1852. "The Moorings," the only Blair mansion still standing, is in Jesup Blair Park.

Francis Preston Blair was the first Silver Spring resident to play a role in the Civil War. At Lincoln's behest, Blair met with then U.S. Army colonel Robert E. Lee on April 18, 1861, to offer him command of the Union army. The war had begun only two days earlier with the Confederate attack on Fort Sumter. Lee's home state, Virginia, had seceded from the Union the following day. Lee didn't accept Blair's offer, and two days later, he resigned his commission. Soon

The Acorn gazebo near the spring on Francis Preston Blair's "Silver Spring" estate still stands in Acorn Park, 8060 Newell Street, near East– West Highway. *Photo by the author.*

he was leading the Confederate forces. We can only speculate how history might have been different if Blair had been more persuasive.[9]

Francis Preston Blair and his sons were not the only prominent Washingtonians to have mansions or summer homes in the Sligo area. George Washington Riggs also had a country estate in the area. Riggs was one of the founders of a brokerage and banking firm that financed U.S. participation in the Mexican-American War. The bank evolved to become the Riggs National Bank, the largest and most prestigious bank in Washington. Lincoln had an account there during the Civil War, and in 1867, the bank supplied $7.2 million in gold bullion to the U.S. government

Montgomery Blair, Francis Preston Blair's son and Lincoln's postmaster general. *Library of Congress.*

to purchase Alaska from Russia. In 1857 and 1858, Riggs purchased three parcels totaling 147 acres stretching from Georgia Avenue on the west to beyond Sligo Creek on the east and from Colesville Road on the north to Bonifant Street on the south. In 1858, he built his home at the end of a long drive off Georgia Avenue. Pershing Drive was originally part of the lane leading to his home, which still stands at 711 Pershing Drive in Seven Oaks–Evanswood. Before moving to Silver Spring, Riggs built and lived in the thirty-two-room house used as a summer home by Lincoln during the war and now known as "President Lincoln's Cottage" on his 256-acre estate, which became the Soldiers' Home and is now the Armed Forces Retirement Home. Like Francis Preston Blair, Riggs was a slave owner. In 1862, when slaves were freed in the District of Columbia, Riggs submitted a claim to the government for $1,500 (equivalent to a little more than $34,000 in 2014) for the loss of the services of his two slaves.[10]

Francis Preston Blair's and George Washington Riggs' estates were quite different from the working farms of their less wealthy neighbors. At least in Blair's case, their politics were quite different, too. Not only was Blair a Republican, he was a very well-connected Republican opposed to secession. Most other Sligo-area residents definitely were not Republicans, but they were split on the secession issue; even individual families were divided on this issue.

The Blair family's immediate neighbors to the north were the Wilson family, who owned the farm on both sides of Georgia Avenue north of Sligo and ten slaves. Like most area residents, Thomas Noble Wilson and his son Richard T. Wilson favored secession, but son John C. Wilson opposed it. The issue was extremely divisive. As early as 1856, there had been an effort to remove Francis Preston Blair from the board of the Montgomery County Agricultural Society because he opposed secession even if secession was the only way to preserve slavery.[11]

Today, Silver Spring is considered a near suburb of Washington. In the 1860s, Washington was a much more distant presence linked to Silver Spring only by the Seventh Street Turnpike (then also referred to as the Seventh Street Pike or Seventh Street Road and now Georgia Avenue). The Metropolitan Branch of the Baltimore & Ohio (B&O) Railroad through Silver Spring and Montgomery County would not be completed until 1873. The city of Washington, which had a population of 61,112 in 1860, extended north only to today's Florida Avenue and no farther east than the Anacostia River. Georgetown had another 8,733 people. The remainder of the District of Columbia ("Washington County") was a rural area with a population of only 5,225. Free blacks made up almost 15 percent of the population. Slaves were just over 4 percent.[12]

Even though the city of Washington was the fourteenth-largest city in the country, its population was less than a third that of Baltimore and only about one-seventeenth that of New York City with Brooklyn.[13] It was not exactly what we would think of today as urban. Livestock roamed unpaved streets and empty squares. Poorly drained canals were essentially open sewers. The Capitol and Washington Monument were unfinished, and other relatively grand government buildings seemed out of place among the city's other buildings.[14]

Chapter 3

THE CIVIL WAR COMES TO
SILVER SPRING

1861–1863

A s Southern states began seceding in December 1860 and January 1861, the Federal government took steps to ensure that Montgomery County and all of Maryland remained under Union control. Ultimately, Maryland's secession was prevented when Federal troops accompanied by Baltimore City Police—Baltimore by this time was under firm Federal control—went to Frederick, where the special secession convention was to take place on September 17, 1861. The troops had orders to arrest any delegates who were pro-secession. Maryland remained in the Union.[15]

Almost as soon as the war began in April 1861, the Union set up a series of observation posts throughout southern Montgomery County to report any secessionist activities and provide a warning of Confederate raids. By June 11, Union forces had set up a headquarters in Rockville. The first skirmish of the war in a "Northern" state took place between local Confederates and Union troops where Seneca Creek empties into the Potomac on June 14. Union troops built several blockhouses along the Potomac River to protect the Chesapeake & Ohio (C&O) Canal and prevent Confederate raiders from coming into the county. Signal towers and telegraph lines were also built.[16]

Union troops in Montgomery County encouraged slaves to go with the army and took livestock for food and fencing for firewood. At least one Wilson family slave was among those who left early in the war. In July 1861, Thomas Noble Wilson asked his neighbor Francis Preston Blair for help in recovering him. Given the Blair family's well-known anti-abolition views, it is not surprising that Wilson asked for the favor and that

Blair complied. Blair gave Wilson the following letter of introduction to President Lincoln:[17]

> *Silver Spring*
> *9 July '61*
>
> *Dear Sir:*
> *My neighbor Mr Wilson, (a respectable farmer) has a boy (Negro) with one of the Maine Regiments in Va & asks a letter of introduction to you to ascertain to whom he is to apply for his recovery—I have given him this note that he may receive what ever you may deem fit to be communicated on the subject—*
>
> *Yo. mo. ob. st*
> *F.P. Blair*

Whether Lincoln assisted Wilson is unknown, but it appears that Wilson did not recover the slave.

The first skirmish in the Silver Spring area took place on November 27, 1861. Company B of the First New Jersey Cavalry, which had only recently been assigned to a new camp near Georgia Avenue north of Florida Avenue, sent a scouting expedition north to Silver Spring. The *New York Times* reported, "A small party was sent forward, who on reaching the summit of a hill were met by a party of the enemy. A brisk exchange of shots ensued, and our men formed in a line of battle and prepared to advance, but the enemy fell back."[18] Just who the enemy was is unclear.

Although Union patrols and scouting expeditions likely continued, the first major troop movement through the area came about ten months later. In early September 1862, Generals Ambrose Burnside and Joseph Hooker led Union troops up Georgia Avenue past Silver Spring and through Olney and Brookeville toward Darnestown and Poolesville, where Confederate troops under Robert E. Lee had captured Union cavalry elements. They finally caught up with the Confederates at the Battle of Antietam near Sharpsburg, Maryland, on September 17.

Troop movements up Georgia Avenue were a major concern to local residents. Female parishioners petitioned General Burnside not to harm Grace Church. Burnside not only ensured his troops did not harm the church, but he also sent a contribution to help pay for the still unbuilt roof. The fact that Postmaster General Montgomery Blair was a patron of the new church may have influenced Burnside's action.

This is the only known drawing of the first Grace Church building, which was completed during the Civil War and burned in 1896. It was described as "a modest structure roofed with chestnut shingles, and painted light brown." It had a large granite block in front of the door, a large stained-glass window and a gallery at the back for slaves. (Detail from Montgomery County Plat #15, "Kingsville," June 1895.) *Maryland State Archives.*

Union pickets patrolled the Silver Spring area, as well as other parts of Montgomery County. Their primary purpose may have been to keep an area largely made up of Southern sympathizers under control. Sometimes they needed to control marauding by other soldiers as well. One example involved the death of Thomas Noble Wilson. The *Evening Star* of September 19, 1862, reported:

MURDER IN MONTGOMERY COUNTY—Yesterday afternoon three soldiers belonging to the 22d Massachusetts regiment went on the farm of a Mr. [Thomas Noble] Wilson, near Silver Spring, and attempted to steal some of his pigs, but the old gentleman discovering them expostulated with them, and at last attempted to pull a pig away from them, when he was knocked down and run through the body with a bayonet by one of the party, from the effects of which wounds he died in a short time. In the course of the afternoon one of the party, named John Mara [Marra], *was arrested and taken to Fort Massachusetts* [later renamed Fort Stevens], *and was turned over by Major Sadler, commanding the fort, to* [police] *Officer Malloy, who brought him to the Central Guardhouse.*[19]

A week later, the *Montgomery County Sentinel* in a story headlined "Another Murder by Soldiers" mostly copied the *Star* item but added a few new details and omitted the arrest. The *Sentinel* reported that "the old gentleman" had been "knocked from his horse and baynoted [*sic*] through the neck by one of the party, from the effects of which wound, he died the next morning. Mr. Wilson was one of our most respectable and enterprising farmers, and highly esteemed by all who knew him."[20]

It is unclear why the army turned Marra over to the civil authorities in Washington, D.C., when the murder took place in Montgomery County, but they did. The *Evening Star* of September 24, 1862, listed under "Police Matters—Second Precinct" "John Mara [Marra], Murder" and said he was held over for a further hearing. Just above the listing for John Mara was "W.H. Rafferty, accessory to murder." Rafferty was also held over for a further hearing but was tried by the army in a court-martial proceeding. There was no mention of a third soldier.

John Marra was a forty-two-year-old private from Sturbridge, Massachusetts, who had been a farmer before joining the army in 1861. He deserted from Company K of the Twenty-second Massachusetts Regiment on September 12, 1862, six days before Wilson's murder.[21] He may have deserted on the way to Antietam. On November 4, he was taken to the Old Capitol Prison, where he was held pending his trial. The trial never took place; Marra escaped at about 8:30 p.m. on January 3, 1863, and was not recaptured. In 1870, he was living in Worcester, Massachusetts, with his wife and two children. He died in 1890.[22]

William H. Rafferty was a twenty-two-year-old private in Company K. He had been a fireworks maker in Cambridge, Massachusetts, before joining the army.[23] He started toward Antietam with his regiment but became ill and was left to return to Washington on his own. Rafferty was charged with being AWOL and with "plunder and pillage," but he claimed to have been at Wilson's house getting water and talking to the family when the murder took place.[24]

According to testimony in Rafferty's court-martial, three soldiers, including one with a yellow handkerchief, were walking along the fence separating Thomas Noble Wilson's field from the west side of Georgia Avenue about sixty to one hundred yards north of Wilson's house. One of them shot a hog in the field. The hog didn't die immediately, and the soldier with the gun went over the fence to catch it and finish it off. This was witnessed by Hanson Smith, an eighteen-year-old slave owned by Wilson, who was on horseback returning from the stores in Sligo, and W.H. Giddons, who was working on the farm. Smith immediately rode to the house and told Wilson that soldiers were killing his hogs. The seventy-one-year-old Wilson, who was sitting on the porch, got on the horse and rode out to confront the soldiers. Giddons, too, headed toward the Wilson house but on his way was met by Wilson riding toward the scene with Smith following on foot. When Wilson got to the fence, he tied the horse and headed toward the soldier who had his hog. When he got to within about three yards of him, one of the group hit him with a gun, knocking him to the ground. Another soldier then "bayoneted him three or four times in the neck" while the soldier who had shot the hog yelled "hit him" and "kill the son of a bitch." Smith ran back to the house saying, "The soldiers killed Massa!" People from the house chased one soldier who was running toward Washington, but they lost sight of him when they reached the top of a hill with woods on both sides. The alarm was raised, and two soldiers were arrested by pickets stationed at the tollgate just south of Colesville Road in Sligo. Contrary to the story in the *Sentinel*, Wilson died within about a half hour of being bayoneted.[25]

Rafferty was acquitted despite testimony from Hanson Smith identifying him. There was doubt whether Smith's testimony was accurate, since other witnesses, including Giddons, were either unable to identify Rafferty or said they had seen him at the Wilson house at the time of the murder. There was also testimony that Rafferty was on the "sick list" and not AWOL. Rafferty continued to serve in the army until he was discharged for disability (defective vision in his right eye related to iritis) in April 1864. He returned to Cambridge, Massachusetts, and worked as a shoemaker. He died from tuberculosis in 1871.[26]

At least some of the confusion about Rafferty resulted from another incident that had taken place at Samuel Cissle's home, a little north of the Wilson home on Georgia Avenue, just before Wilson was killed. Mr. Cissle testified in Rafferty's court-martial that the group of soldiers who were involved in Wilson's murder had come to his home asking for something to eat. He gave them some food. He testified that they "started to go away and they shot some of my turkeys and chickens, and one attempted to shoot me while I was standing in the door. He aimed at me, and I dodged behind the door." He also said that one of the soldiers stole a coffee mill from his kitchen. While being held, Rafferty was found to have a coffee mill wrapped in a yellow handkerchief, which would seem highly incriminating, but Rafferty claimed to have acquired the items from another soldier. The jury apparently believed him and the witnesses who said he was at the Wilson home at the time of the murder.[27]

The Wilson family had other problems in addition to Thomas Nobel Wilson's murder. On November 15, Richard T. Wilson and his brother-in-law Lewis Magruder, acting as Thomas Noble Wilson's executors, began running ads in the *Evening Star* specifying a $150 (equivalent to about $3,400 in 2014) reward for the return of three runaway slaves or a $50 reward for the return of each slave to the Wilson farm. The slaves were Jasper Detton, about twenty-one years old; Moses Whitecan, about twenty-three years old, "knock kneed, and very much disfigured by the same"; and Lucy Clark, about forty years old and "pleasant when spoken to."[28] It is unlikely that either Detton or Whitecan was the slave about whom Wilson had requested Lincoln's assistance the previous year. All Maryland slaves would be freed less than two years later on November 1, 1864, the effective date of an amendment to the state constitution abolishing slavery that had been narrowly adopted by the voters.[29]

Settling Thomas Noble Wilson's estate also led them to entanglement with the Orphans Court. Apparently, his land had been divided in Wilson's will but not his personal property. In the *Evening Star* issues of November 14 and 26, 1862, the executors advertised a December 2 public auction "on the farm seven miles from Washington" of the late Thomas Noble Wilson's personal property: "Seven Negroes, Horses, Cattle, 2,000 weight of Pork, Provender [animal fodder]; one Rockaway [a type of carriage], Wagons and Carts, Farming Utensils, and Household and Kitchen Furniture, &c."[30]

As might be expected, the murder, the runaways and the auction of property to settle the estate upset the Wilson family, possibly to the extent that some family members considered selling out and moving west. Elizabeth Blair Lee, who was living at her father's "Silver Spring" mansion, wrote to her husband, naval officer Samuel Phillips Lee, on November 25: "Father went all over the Wilson's land today—some of them want to sell and invest in Missouri as that will soon be a free state. They are offered by some northern people 30 dollars an acre. There are between 2 & 3 thousand acres. If sold to northern men in small farms, it will be a good thing for the region."[31] The

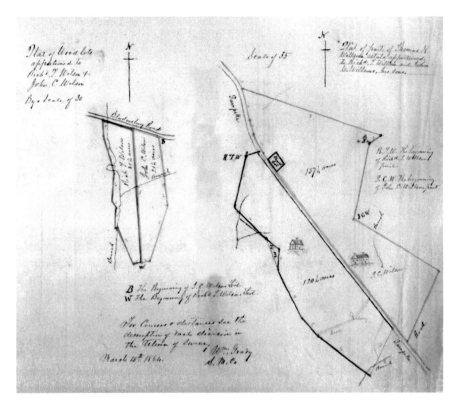

Division of the Wilson farm between sons John C. Wilson and Richard T. Wilson after Thomas Noble Wilson's murder. The drawing on the right shows the farm near Sligo. "Turnpike" is Georgia Avenue. "Road" at lower right is Colesville Road. The parcel on the left side of the sheet was off University Boulevard ("Bladensburg Road"). *Montgomery County Land Records, liber EBP 7, folio 432a.*

Wilson farm would have been a natural addition to Blair's holdings. The boundary between the two farms was about 110 feet south of and parallel to today's Fidler Lane from Georgia Avenue west to the CSX tracks. The Wilsons decided not to sell.

Union troops remained in the area protecting Washington, but not necessarily Sligo-area residents, for the remainder of the war. Life went on normally for the most part. For example, Grace Church got its roof. Elizabeth Blair Lee wrote to her husband on January 17, 1863, that "Mr. Speakman was here today and says our neighbors have again rallied to the unfinished church, which is to be completed by April."[32]

One scare came in June 1863. Lee's army crossed into Maryland on its way to Pennsylvania before it was ultimately turned back at the Battle of Gettysburg on July 3. There were reports that Rebel scouts had been seen near Georgetown, as well as other reports of Rebels in the immediate Washington area. J.E.B. Stuart's cavalry captured about 125 Union supply wagons and passed through Rockville on June 28 on the way to join Lee in Pennsylvania. Some of Stuart's riders went farther afield in Montgomery County. According to the next day's *Evening Star*, "Some of them skirted as near Washington as Silver Spring on the Seventh Street road, but left again in considerable haste." The *Star* also noted, "It is believed that some Marylanders have joined the ranks of the raiders for the nonce [time being], swelling their numbers considerably and making themselves useful as guides from their knowledge of the country and the locality of good stock...Numbers of the farmers in Montgomery are on their way here [Washington], driving their horses and cattle before them."[33] The Confederate threat was taken seriously in Washington.[34] Francis Preston Blair and Postmaster General Montgomery Blair took no chances. On the evening of June 28, they fled their "Silver Spring" and "Falkland" mansions for the safety of the Blair house on Pennsylvania Avenue.[35]

The only major threat came a year later in the summer of 1864.

Chapter 4

PRELUDE TO GENERAL EARLY'S ARRIVAL IN SILVER SPRING

May–July 1864

In May 1864, General Ulysses S. Grant's Army of the Potomac had begun advancing on Richmond, Virginia. After the Battles of the Wilderness and Spotsylvania Court House, Grant moved toward the Cold Harbor crossroads about ten miles northeast of Richmond. He pulled both raw recruits and artillery forces from the defense of Washington for reinforcements. The ensuing battle in early June was a major Union defeat. Grant lost about twelve thousand men killed and wounded and made no progress toward the Confederate capital. However, the continuing presence of Grant's army kept most of the Confederate army bottled up defending Richmond.

General Robert E. Lee wanted to relieve the pressure on Richmond and get his army out of its defensive posture. He also wanted to drive Union troops out of the Shenandoah Valley, which was an important source of agricultural produce for Richmond. He developed a plan to send troops west and north through the Shenandoah Valley and then into Maryland to harass Baltimore, cut Washington off from the north, capture the capital and even free thousands of Confederate prisoners at the Union's prisoner of war camp at Point Lookout, where the Potomac River meets the Chesapeake Bay. Even if not fully successful, the effort would require Grant to divert forces to defend Washington and thereby relieve the pressure on Richmond.

As ordered by Lee, Lieutenant General Jubal Early and his troops left Richmond on June 13, 1864. They headed west into the Shenandoah Valley. Union forces under Major General David Hunter occupying the valley were more interested in avoiding battle than holding the area and did more retreating

Lieutenant General Jubal Early, CSA. *Library of Congress.*

than fighting. On June 18, Lee telegraphed Early that "Grant in front of Petersburg…Strike as quick as you can."[36] General Early headed north to Winchester, arriving there on July 2.[37]

Early and Lee considered but discarded a plan to attack Washington directly from the west through Loudoun and Fairfax Counties. They concluded that this was impractical because they lacked supplies for their troops and animals. As Early later put it, "My provisions were nearly exhausted, and if I had moved through Loudon [*sic*] it would have been necessary for me to halt and thresh wheat and have it ground, as neither bread nor flour could otherwise be obtained, which would have caused much greater delay than was required on the other route [north to Martinsburg and Hagerstown], where we could take provisions from the enemy. Moreover, unless the B&O Railroad was torn up the enemy would have been able to move troops from the west over that road to Washington [by way of Baltimore]."[38]

Early's army went north almost unopposed to Martinsburg, West Virginia, and then to Hagerstown, Middletown and Frederick, Maryland, capturing supplies, including those stored in Union warehouses, as they went. Early demanded and was paid ransoms for not burning the towns: $20,000 from Hagerstown (this amount only because a zero was inadvertently left out of the ransom instructions), $1,500 from Middletown and $200,000 from Frederick.[39]

Early's drive north and the lack of significant opposition caused concern in Pennsylvania and New York, more for their own safety than that of Washington. The two states called out twenty-four thousand militiamen in case Early went farther north. These troops were not sent to Washington.[40]

Meanwhile in Montgomery County, suspected Southern sympathizers were being arrested and taken to Washington. On Sunday, June 26, ten people, including prominent Southern sympathizer Alfred Ray of the "Highlands" (a large estate extending from the grounds of the Mormon Temple, 9900 Stoneybrook Drive, to south of the Beltway and east to the former Walter Reed Annex on Linden Lane), were arrested. The others were "the two Messers. Noland; Benjamin Duvall; William T. Baker; Thomas Beckwith; Henry Warring, Esq."; and "three of the Messrs. Horner." Three of them (Warring and two of the Horners) had also been arrested and jailed eight days earlier but released after a few days. They were taken to the Old Capitol Prison. Most were promptly released, but Ray was held until August 23, when he took the Oath of Allegiance. Reportedly, Francis Preston Blair had pressed for his release. The arrests were probably unrelated to nervousness about Early's intentions.[41]

As late as July 3, when Early's troops had reached Martinsburg, West Virginia, Grant had no idea of what was going on. On that day, he sent a message from his headquarters at City Point, Virginia, to Secretary of War Edwin M. Stanton saying Early's "corps is now here" and posed no threat to Union general Hunter's forces in the Shenandoah Valley![42] Indeed, Grant did not recognize that Confederate forces had crossed into Maryland until July 5, after Early had taken Harpers Ferry and cut the railroad and telegraph lines.

Even then, Grant apparently did not think the invasion amounted to much of a threat to Washington. He authorized sending Brigadier General James B. Ricketts and the Sixth Corps dismounted cavalry and an infantry division "which will be followed by the balance of the corps, *if necessary*" back north.[43] They arrived in Baltimore in time to be taken by train to fight in the Battle of Monocacy on July 9.

Washington was lightly defended by raw recruits; Grant had shifted most of the veteran troops who had been defending Washington to bolster his efforts against Richmond. Army chief of staff major general Henry W. Halleck in Washington had further depleted the defenses by sending some Ohio militia

Edwin M. Stanton, Lincoln's secretary of war. *Library of Congress.*

Major General Henry W. Halleck, USA, chief of staff during General Early's raid on Washington. *Library of Congress.*

troops and dismounted cavalry and light artillery armed as infantry to Harpers Ferry and some cavalry troops to Point of Rocks. Halleck told Grant that the militia defending Washington could "scarcely fire a gun"; he wanted Grant to return a regiment of heavy artillery troops to mix with them. The troops guarding Chain Bridge did not even know how to load their artillery pieces.[44]

Early's forces arrived outside Frederick on Thursday, July 7, complete with long supply wagon trains, livestock and Union prisoners. The livestock and much of the supplies in the wagon trains had been taken from Maryland farms they had passed through. Early proceeded to occupy Frederick and burn all government buildings except for hospitals.[45]

Early also sent a 1,500-man cavalry brigade under the command of Brigadier General Bradley T. Johnson east with the goals of threatening Baltimore, cutting the railroad and telegraph lines from Baltimore to Philadelphia and Washington and freeing the Confederate prisoners at the Point Lookout prisoner of war camp. Johnson was born in Frederick and in 1861 had organized the Confederate army's First Maryland Regiment. His forces raided north and west of Baltimore and then turned south. They arrived at Beltsville on the main road and B&O Railroad line from Washington to Baltimore on Sunday, July 10. At Beltsville, they took about seven hundred mules owned by the government. On July 11, they were ordered to move toward Bladensburg to augment the attack on Washington rather than go on to Point Lookout.[46] Richmond newspapers had printed stories about the planned raid on the POW camp, so Lee called it off, fearing the Union army and navy would be ready for the no-longer-surprise attack.

Early's real target was Washington, not Baltimore or Point Lookout's prisoners. He planned to move his main army down what is now Route 355 to Rockville and then Washington, where he could seize the capital and the huge quantity of military supplies in Washington. The symbolic nature of the victory would be even more valuable to the Confederacy than the military stores.

Even with Early's forces as close as Frederick County, there was still confusion at the highest levels of government. Secretary of the Navy Gideon Welles, who was one of Postmaster General Montgomery Blair's few friends in Lincoln's cabinet, wrote in his diary on Friday, July 8:

[Secretary of War Edwin M.] *Stanton tells me that he has no idea the Rebels are in any force above, and should not give them a serious thought, but Grant says he thinks they are in force, without, however giving his reasons or any facts. The President has been a good deal incredulous about a very large army on the upper Potomac, yet he begins to manifest anxiety. But he is under constraint, I perceive, such as I know is sometimes imposed by the dunderheads at the War Office, when they are in a fog, or scare, and know not what to say or do. It is not natural or the way of the President to withhold information, or speculate at such times, and I can always tell how things are with Halleck and Stanton when there are important movements going on. The President is now enjoined to silence, while Halleck is in a perfect maze, bewildered, without intelligent decision or self-reliance, and Stanton is wisely ignorant. I am inclined to believe, however, that at this time profound ignorance reigns at the War Department concerning the Rebel raid in the Shenandoah Valley; that they absolutely know nothing of it,—its numbers, where it is, or its destination. It has to me appeared more mischievous than to others. I think we are in no way prepared for it, and a fierce onset could not well be resisted. It is doubtful, however, whether the onset will be made, for it is the nature of man to lose his opportunities. The true course of the Rebels is to strike at once at this point.*[47]

There was confusion and nervousness in Silver Spring, too. Elizabeth Blair Lee wrote to her husband on July 8. As the possibility of an invasion loomed, she was about to leave for Cape May, New Jersey, with her mother. Her father, Francis Preston Blair, and brother, Postmaster General Montgomery Blair, were leaving for a long-planned two-week hunting and

Gideon Welles, Lincoln's secretary of the navy. *Library of Congress.*

fishing trip to Pennsylvania with two of Francis Preston Blair's grandsons. She wrote that some family members said they heard cannon all day on the seventh but that others said it was thunder. She also wrote that Assistant Navy Secretary Gustavus Fox, who was Montgomery Blair's brother-in-law, had told them that Early had given up and had retreated back down the valley, but "others insist the enemy are 40,000 strong. The silence of the officials is ominous to me, and I am glad to go where I can sleep more than I can here."[48]

The next day in his diary, Gideon Welles continued to express puzzlement about what was going on: "The Blairs have left, strangely, it appears to me, at this time, on a fishing excursion among the mountain streams of interior Pennsylvania, and the ladies have hastily run off from Silver Spring to Cape May, leaving their premises at a critical moment."[49]

Meanwhile in Baltimore, Union major general Lew Wallace (later the author of *Ben-Hur*), whose troops were guarding that city, had received reports that the Confederates were marching on Frederick. Wallace had been relegated to defending Baltimore because of his supposed incompetence at Shiloh. Baltimore was not thought to be a likely Confederate target, and his troops were not much better than the ones that had been left to defend Washington. Nevertheless, putting a very liberal interpretation on his orders to defend Baltimore, Wallace sent his troops west to Frederick to meet Early's advance. His forces briefly occupied Frederick, but as Early approached the city on the night of Friday, July 8, they fell back to the Monocacy River, where they could block the roads to both Baltimore and Washington and could be reinforced from Baltimore via the B&O Railroad. Ultimately, he had about six thousand men to face Early's force, which was estimated by some to have increased to twenty thousand or more.[50]

Wallace's defensive stand on the south side of the Monocacy River kept Early from advancing toward Washington all day Saturday, July 9. At about 5:00 p.m., after three successive Confederate attacks, Wallace's forces were outflanked and forced to withdraw back toward Baltimore. They were greeted by a large crowd at Camden Station when their thirty-two-car, two-locomotive train arrived. Almost a quarter of his troops didn't make the trip; they had been killed or were wounded or missing.[51]

Major General Lew Wallace, USA. *Library of Congress.*

Although his outnumbered troops lost the Battle of Monocacy, Wallace's action to delay Early probably saved Washington by giving Grant enough time to move more reinforcements up from the Richmond area. Wallace's reward was to be relieved of his command on Sunday, July 10, because he had lost the battle.[52] He was reinstated to his command on July 28 by Secretary of War Stanton.[53]

In time, Lincoln came to recognize Wallace's contribution, at least indirectly. After Early had retreated from Washington, Lincoln sent a letter to John W. Garrett, president of the B&O Railroad (and for whom the Montgomery County town of Garrett Park on the B&O's Metropolitan Branch was later named), saying Garrett was "the right arm of the Federal Government in the aid he rendered the authorities in preventing the Confederates from seizing Washington and securing its retention as the Capital of the Loyal States."[54] That aid was primarily moving Wallace's troops to and from Frederick and the Monocacy battleground.

While Wallace was delaying Early at the Battle of Monocacy, Grant finally recognized there was some danger to Washington. Even so, he apparently did not understand what was really happening. He wired Major General Halleck in Washington at 6:00 p.m. on Saturday, July 9, that "forces enough to defeat all that Early has with him should get to his rear south of him

[Early's rear was actually to the north!], and follow him up sharply, leaving him to go north, defending depots, towns, &c, with small garrisons and the militia."[55] Both Lincoln and Halleck reacted to this with skepticism. Lincoln wired Grant at 2:00 p.m. the next afternoon suggesting that Grant come with troops to defend Washington:

> *General Halleck says we have absolutely no force here fit to go to the field. He thinks that with the 100-days' men and invalids we have here we can defend Washington, and scarcely Baltimore. Besides these there are about 8,000, not very reliable, under Howe, at Harper's Ferry, with Hunter approaching that point very slowly, and with what number I suppose you know better than I. Wallace, with some odds and ends and part of what came up with Ricketts, was so badly beaten yesterday at Monocacy that what is left can attempt no more than to defend Baltimore. What we shall get in from Pennsylvania and New York will scarcely be worth counting, I fear. Now what I think is that you should provide to retain your hold where you are, certainly, and bring the rest with you personally, and make a vigorous effort to destroy the enemy's force in this vicinity. I think there is really a fair chance to do this if the movement is prompt. That is what I think, upon your suggestion, and is not an order.*[56]

Halleck responded to Grant at 9:30 p.m. on Sunday, July 10, seven hours after Lincoln's response, with even less confidence than Lincoln had displayed, if that is possible:

> *Your telegram of 6 p.m. yesterday is received. Whether you had better come here or remain there is a question upon which I cannot advise. What you say about getting into Early's rear is perfectly correct, but unfortunately we have no forces here for the field. All such forces were sent to you long ago. What we have here are raw militia, invalids, convalescents from the hospitals, a few dismounted batteries, and the dismounted and disorganized cavalry sent up from James River. With these we expect to defend our immense depots of stores and the line of entrenchments around the city; but what can we do with such forces in the field against a column of 20,000 veterans? One-half of the men cannot march at all. The only men fit for the field was Ricketts' division, which has been defeated and badly cut up under Wallace...We are impressing horses to remount the cavalry. It arrives destitute of everything; there is necessary delay in preparing it for service.*[57]

Grant had authorized sending the two remaining divisions of the Sixth Corps back to Washington before he received Lincoln's and Halleck's messages, but he declined to go back to Washington himself. He telegraphed Lincoln that "it would do no good" for him to go and it would have a "bad effect" if he left his siege headquarters at City Point.[58]

The two Sixth Corps divisions left around 11:00 p.m. on Saturday, July 9, for a fourteen-mile march to City Point, where they were to board boats waiting for them on the James River for the trip to Washington. They hadn't been told where they were going and had "no idea that one Jubal Early was on the warpath in Maryland with his corps of seasoned veterans, and that the 6th corps was pulling up its shelter tents to get on his trail," as one soldier recalled in his memoirs. Instead, they speculated that they were being sent to attack Wilmington, North Carolina; put down riots in New York City; or even join the army in the West.[59] They arrived at City Point around daylight and eventually were loaded onto boats Sunday evening for the trip down the James River into the Chesapeake Bay and then up the Potomac.

Meanwhile in Washington, Quartermaster General Montgomery C. Meigs wasn't waiting for Grant's troops to arrive. Although he expected Early to retreat rather than attack Washington, he was taking no chances. While the Monocacy fighting was going on, he organized about 1,500 civilian quartermaster employees into an ad-hoc defensive force and armed them.[60] This wasn't the first time civilian employees had been mobilized into military companies when Washington was thought to be threatened. They had first been mobilized after the Second Battle of Bull Run in 1862.[61]

More real troops were also soon on the way. On Monday, July 11, the first ships carrying a full division of the Nineteenth Corps, which Grant had ordered to Virginia from Louisiana, arrived at City Point. They had left New Orleans eight days earlier for the voyage across the Gulf of Mexico, around Florida, up the East Coast, into the Chesapeake Bay and then up the James River. Grant sent them back down the James and then to Washington.[62]

Chapter 5

ON TO ROCKVILLE! PANIC IN WASHINGTON!

Sunday, July 10, 1864

July 10 would have been a quiet Sunday in Montgomery County if it hadn't been for Early's invasion. Aside from the war itself, the only thing out of the ordinary was that local farmers had started cutting their wheat earlier than usual because of the war-induced labor shortage. The crop was "far short of an average one," however, probably because of the extended unusually hot and dry weather.[63] Even so, the countryside was described as a "veritable paradise" by a Union prisoner forced to march with Early's troops from Frederick toward Rockville.[64]

The poor condition of the wheat crop was not the primary concern on most people's minds that day. Early's movement into Maryland and his success at Hagerstown and Frederick had prompted considerable concern among local residents, to put it mildly. Visitors in Washington were reportedly "very frightened and were very anxious to leave town in the first train."[65] The safety of train travel, however, was questionable since the Confederates raided the Western Maryland Railroad near Union Bridge (about twenty miles northeast of Frederick) and roughly twelve miles farther east at Westminster (about thirty miles northwest of Baltimore). They also destroyed bridges and took control of the Northern Central Railroad near Timonium (about ten miles north of downtown Baltimore).[66]

By early Sunday morning, Wallace realized that Early had not seriously pursued his defeated forces as they retreated to Baltimore. He concluded that Early would move toward Washington. At 6:40 a.m., he warned army headquarters in Washington. His telegram said: "I have been defeated…the enemy are not pursuing me, from which I infer they are marching on Washington."[67]

Wallace's assessment of where Early was going wasn't universally shared, however. At 5:30 a.m., Lieutenant Amos M. Thayer, a signal officer who had established a station on Catoctin Mountain, had sent a probably less than helpful dispatch saying, "The enemy's forces have left Frederick and are now all across the Monocacy River…They are either marching on Washington or Baltimore, or are retreating toward Edwards Ferry."[68]

Wallace had it right. Early was advancing on Washington. Early later said that he didn't pursue Wallace because he didn't want to capture a lot of prisoners. Nevertheless, he did capture between six and seven hundred men, most of whom were taken with the army on to Washington and then back into Virginia and eventually to a POW camp.[69]

The Union troops guarding the forts north of Washington were put on heightened alert. Brush was cleared in front of the forts. Artillery was shot as practice. No one was permitted to leave his post.[70]

About five to eight hundred Union cavalry troops, including some regulars, were pulled together at Falls Church and then sent north from Washington toward Early's advancing forces. They could do little but harass the Confederates, and by 4:00 p.m., their commander informed headquarters that his rear guard was "fighting the enemy near Rockville." He also suggested that the forts north of Washington be "strongly guarded."[71]

Assistant Secretary of the Navy Gustavus Fox ordered preparations for President Lincoln to escape by boat down the Potomac. When Lincoln learned of this, he was "greatly discomposed and annoyed."[72]

The Smithsonian was also taking precautions. Solomon Brown, the Smithsonian's first black employee, was ordered to dig a hole so the institution's valuables could be buried if necessary to keep them out of Confederate hands.[73]

These actions may have been at least somewhat justified. Advance troops from Early's forces had apparently arrived near Georgetown, although the War Department was unaware of the fact. Confederate brigadier general John McCausland later claimed that he had briefly occupied an undefended fort, probably Fort Gaines, which was near the intersection of today's Nebraska and New Mexico Avenues.[74] Secretary of the Navy Gideon Welles recorded in his diary:

When at the Department, Sunday morning, examining my mail, one of the clerks came in and stated that the Rebel pickets were on the outskirts of Georgetown, within the District lines. There had been no information to warn us of this near approach of the enemy, but my informant was so positive—and soon confirmed by another—that I sent to the War Department to ascertain the facts. They were ignorant—had heard street rumors, but they were unworthy of notice—and ridiculed my inquiry.[75]

He also noted that the son of one of his neighbors had been captured by the Rebel pickets inside the District of Columbia and was being held prisoner.[76]

Besides the telegrams from Lincoln and Halleck, there were other calls for Grant and others to send troops to Washington. The assistant secretary of war wired General Grant that both Baltimore and Washington "are in a great state of panic" and both cities were "filled with country people fleeing from the enemy."[77] Troops were also requested from the north. The Union commander in Philadelphia was directed to "send forward to Baltimore all convalescents fit for duty, armed or unarmed as may [be] most expeditious."[78]

Despite the pleas, Grant was not overly concerned about the threats to Washington and Baltimore. His adjutant general told a Boston reporter that Early's movements in Maryland "will not affect operations here [before Richmond]. Lee undoubtedly expected to send Grant post-haste to Washington; but the siege will go on."[79]

While Washington and Baltimore were in a "great state of panic," President Lincoln was trying to maintain calm, but apparently he wasn't too confident. In response to a call from Baltimore for troops to be sent there from Washington, he replied, "I have not a single soldier but who is being disposed by the military for the best protection of all...Let us be vigilant but keep cool. I hope neither Baltimore nor Washington will be taken."[80]

All was definitely not cool in Baltimore, where "the valuables, records, &c, of our banks and other institutions have been placed on board a steamer in the harbor for safety." The governor of Maryland urgently requested that the mayor of Philadelphia send troops, saying, "Your country requires your immediate service, and the safety of your own soil and your good neighbors in Maryland may depend on your promptness...Come forward like men to aid her. The rebel forces will be easily defeated and driven away if you do your duty; and I pray God to enlighten you that the honor of the Commonwealth [of Pennsylvania] may be maintained." Despite the plea, no one came from Philadelphia to defend Baltimore.[81]

All was not cool in Washington either. On Sunday evening, Secretary of War Stanton sent a carriage to Lincoln's summer "cottage" at the Soldiers' Home (in the countryside a little less than two miles southeast of Fort Stevens) "with positive orders" that Lincoln and his family should be brought back to the White House for their own safety. "Lincoln, very much irritated, and against his will, came back to town," arriving with his family at the White House after midnight.[82]

An army captain who was in Washington at the time, looking back more than twenty years later, said that Sunday, July 10, the day after the Battle of Monocacy, was

> *the blackest Sunday ever known in Washington. Not only the President, but everybody at the capital, down to the raggedest* [sic] *"contraband"* [a slave from a Confederate state who had escaped to Union-held territory] *in the streets, knew that the Confederates had been between the city and the North for a week; that railroad and telegraph communication was cut off; that the city was threatened with famine for lack of supplies; that a battle had been fought near Frederick, the Union forces defeated, and little more than a day's march would bring Early to the northern suburbs... On that Sunday and on the forenoon of the next day, there was not a sadder, more anxious heart in the land than that of Abraham Lincoln. He fully realized the peril of the capital, and facts are stated (which are beyond the knowledge of the present writer) that a vessel was kept ready at the wharf, with steam up, to ensure the escape of the President, cabinet, and other government functionaries should the necessity arise.*[83]

The panic in southern Montgomery County and Washington was justified. General Early arrived in Rockville about 8:00 p.m. on Sunday evening and held a conference with his officers in the county clerk's office at the courthouse (then just west of the current Red Brick Courthouse) to plan for the next day's advance. Meanwhile, various Confederate advance units had not only reached Rockville but had probed south throughout southern Montgomery County and into Washington toward the city's forts. Union troops in the area had fallen back.

As word of the Confederate advance down Route 355 through Urbana, Hyattstown and Clarksburg and toward Rockville spread, refugees began pouring into Washington. *Sacramento Union* correspondent Noah Brooks later recalled:

> *The news of the approach of Early was brought to the city (whatever may have been the information lodged in the War Department) by the panic-stricken people from Rockville, Silver Spring, Tennallytown, and other*

Maryland villages. These people came flocking into Washington by the Seventh street road, flying in wild disorder, and bringing their household goods with them. In a general way we understood that the city was cut off at the north and east, and that the famine of market-stuff, New York newspapers, and other necessities of life, was due to the cutting of railway lines leading northward. For two or three days we had no mail, no telegraphic messages, and no railway travel. Our only communication with the other world was by steamer from Georgetown, D.C. to New York. Washington was in a ferment.[84]

The main body of Confederate troops reached Rockville about 11:00 p.m., but troops camped for the night all along the road between Gaithersburg and Rockville.[85]

Early also slept that night between Gaithersburg and Rockville. After meeting with his officers at the courthouse, Early rode back north and spent the night at John T. DeSellum's "Summit Hall" (now "Bohrer Park at Summit Hall Farm" at 506 South Frederick Avenue) in Gaithersburg. As he left the next day, his troops sacked the farm and stole almost all the grain, leaving only two bags.[86]

Chapter 6
WASHINGTON'S DEFENSES

Early could (and did) march through Montgomery County and Silver Spring, but on paper, at least, he had no realistic chance of advancing much farther. The city of Washington was surrounded by sixty-eight forts and intervening trenches and rifle pits, all of which had been built beginning in May 1861. The fortifications north of the Potomac were mostly in Washington County, the rural area in the District of Columbia surrounding the city of Washington and Georgetown.

The Union loss on July 21, 1861, at the First Battle of Bull Run, which had taken place only about thirty miles from Washington, gave the army a considerable incentive to quickly strengthen and complete the city's defenses. Major General George B. McClellan, who became commander of the Army of the Potomac shortly after the Bull Run debacle, ordered a substantial increase in the effort. The Army of the Potomac's chief engineer, Major General John G. Barnard, explained that "with our army demoralized and too weak in numbers to act effectually in the open field against the invading enemy, nothing but the protection of defensive works could give any degree of security." The land for the forts was simply occupied without regard to the rights of the owners or any compensation to them. Homes, a church and other buildings were demolished. Rifle trenches and military roads were constructed as needed through cultivated fields and orchards. In the fall of 1862, between two and three thousand troops were detailed to clear standing timber up to two miles in front of the new forts.[87]

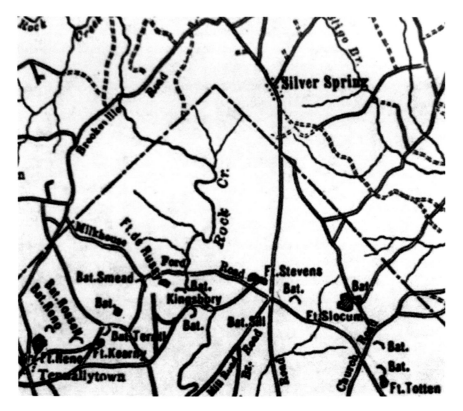

Detail of the Silver Spring and northern District of Columbia area from the War Department Defenses of Washington Map, 1865. *Library of Congress.*

Once completed, Washington's defenses were considered the best line of fortifications in the world. If Early advanced directly south from Rockville, he would face Fort Reno (east of what is now Wisconsin Avenue above Tenleytown) and Forts Bayard and Simmons west toward the Potomac. To the east of Fort Reno, he faced Fort DeRussy (east of today's Oregon Avenue north of Military Road in Rock Creek Park), Fort Stevens (west of Georgia Avenue at Rittenhouse Street), Fort Slocum (near Blair Road and Kansas Avenue in Fort Slocum Park) and Fort Totten (at Fort Totten Drive, just south of Riggs Road). Lesser batteries and other earthworks were set up between the forts. Other forts extended around the city to the east, south and west.

In July 1864, however, the forts amounted to a paper tiger, at least insofar as they were manned. Washington in reality was very lightly defended. In 1861, it had been estimated that 34,125 troops were needed to staff the forts. But in mid-1864, fewer than a third of that number were even in the city, let alone at the forts. Most of the troops in Washington were either medically unfit for combat or raw untrained recruits, and few were stationed at the forts.[88]

In the spring of 1864, most of the veteran troops had been ordered south to reinforce Grant's siege of Richmond. A correspondent for the *New York Herald* who toured the forts on July 11, the day Early arrived, said, "The armament was insufficient, the ordnance supplies were limited, and all... were so weakly manned as to make any protracted resistance impossible."[89] And that assessment had been made one day after the "Veteran Reserve Corps," composed of injured but recuperating soldiers and which had been officially known until only four months earlier as the "Invalid Corps,"[90] had been sent to bolster the defenses at Fort Reno. One of the Veteran Reserve Corps troops confirmed the weakness of the defenses. He said that if Early had attacked the night of July 10–11, the city could not have been saved because his unit had the only available troops and they "were supposed to be unfit for active service."[91]

The army's leadership and command structure was in as much a state of unreadiness as the forts. While there was an under-supply of troops, there was an over-supply of generals, which led to confusion. The line of forts

Battery protecting Chain Bridge, 1862. *Library of Congress.*

was divided into three sections under the command of different generals of differing ranks, all of whom were given their new commands very early on the morning of Monday, July 11. The reserves were under yet another general. Still another general was in charge of the entire line of forts, but he reported to the army's Department of Washington, which was led by a major general. A colonel in the Department of Washington served as the military governor of Washington, and he also had some command authority. In addition, the Corps of Engineers, which had built the forts, returned officers and a major general to the city to help with the defenses.[92]

As General Early advanced toward Washington, he was unaware of just how weakly defended the city was.

Chapter 7

EARLY'S NEXT STOP, SILVER SPRING

Monday, July 11, 1864

G eneral Early returned to Rockville for the second time about 8:00 a.m. on Monday morning, July 11, but elements of his forces continued to be strung out to Gaithersburg and beyond in the blistering heat of one of the hottest Julys in memory. As before, they were accompanied by a long supply train of wagons and about six hundred captured Union troops. One of the prisoners noted in his diary that "Rebs use us well but give us no rations. Kept moving until we reached the defenses, where the rebs are fighting our folks."[93]

Some Union forces went north from Fort Reno to meet a smaller body of Confederates heading toward the fort. They were forced to retreat, and a "small picket" of Union troops on the Rockville road was captured.[94] The Rebels advanced to within about four miles of Tenleytown, near Fort Reno. Nevertheless, shelling from Fort Reno into what is now the National Institutes of Health campus and reconnoitering reports about the area's topography and the forts south of Rockville convinced Early that an attack down the road from Rockville to Georgetown was not the best way to take Washington.

Instead, Early moved most of his army, its supply trains and its prisoners southeast from Rockville down the New Cut road (today's Veirs Mill Road) and then the Seventh Street pike (or road; today's Georgia Avenue) toward Silver Spring. The Seventh Street pike, a somewhat improved toll road, was the main route through the countryside and to the city of Washington below Boundary Street (renamed Florida Avenue in 1890). Fort Stevens lay in his path.

William H. Batchelor, whom Elizabeth Blair Lee described as an "exact Englishman and self made man of business habits and wealth,"[95] saw the Confederate army pass his home on the east side of Georgia Avenue just north of Forest Glen Road. He later said that "the rebels commenced passing his house toward Washington about 9 o'clock Monday morning (July 11). All of the cavalry had not passed until about 12 m. [noon], when they were followed by a body of sappers and miners, or infantry with picks and shovels, and that the infantry and artillery continued to pass constantly until 6 o'clock in the evening, when the rear guard, consisting of the brigades of Generals [John] Echols and [Gabriel C.] Wharton, encamped or bivouacked near his house on the side toward Washington."[96] The army was said to have stretched for nine miles along the road.

Another witness described the Confederate artillery, such as it was: "Mr. Davis, who keeps the toll-gate at Silver Spring, saw the artillery pass his place to Blair's place, where it was parked, and estimates it about twenty pieces."[97]

In his autobiography, Early described his advance from Rockville toward Washington:

> *We moved at daylight on* [Monday] *the 11th; McCausland moving on the Georgetown pike, while the infantry, preceded by* [Brigadier General John D.] *Imboden's cavalry under Colonel* [George H.] *Smith, turned to the left at Rockville, so as to reach the 7th Street pike which runs by Silver Spring into Washington. Jackson's* [foot] *cavalry moved on the left flank. The previous day had been very warm, and the roads were exceedingly dusty, as there had been no rain for several weeks. The heat during the night had been very oppressive, and but little rest had been obtained. This day was an exceedingly hot one, and there was no air stirring. While marching, the men were enveloped in a suffocating cloud of dust, and many of them fell by the way from exhaustion. Our progress was therefore very much impeded, but I pushed on as rapidly as possible, hoping to get into the fortifications around Washington before they could be manned.*[98]

A prisoner offered another account of the march from Rockville toward Washington that Monday:

> *Between Rockville and Washington we were drawn up in line and thoroughly searched. Money was the chief object of rebel cupidity, and all that could be found was seized. In expectation of such an event, the men*

having money had carefully concealed it, so that the net results must have been exceedingly meagre [sic].

The day itself was one of the hottest of a very hot summer, and many, both Federal and Confederate, were overcome by the heat. While traveling this road southeast from Rockville, we saw mortar shells sent up from the defenses, and the curves described by them were most beautiful. Exploding high in the air, at times, they gave a superb display of pyrotechnics, though I must confess that our admiration was somewhat tempered with apprehension least "some droppings might fall on us." To be wounded or killed was not longed for at any time, but certainly we didn't fancy blows from the hands of our friends.

Stereopticon view of Francis Preston Blair's "Silver Spring" mansion, used by General Early as his headquarters. The mansion is shown here with U.S. military guards in late July, a few days after Early's retreat. Note the officer in the window to the left of the standing sentry. *Library of Congress.*

The afternoon was half spent when we filed to our left into an apple orchard and were ordered to camp. We had passed Silver Spring, the home of Montgomery Blair [sic; actually Francis Preston Blair], and from the nearness of the firing I concluded that we were pretty close to the head of Seventh street. I recall very vividly that several times during that afternoon, the early evening and the day following, shells from our own batteries went shrieking through the tops of the trees under which we were lying.[99]

Major General Alexander McDowell McCook was in command of the defending troops and fortifications. As Early's forces approached, he wired the War Department: "The advance cavalry pickets two and a half miles beyond fortifications [i.e., near the later site of Silver Spring's B&O Railroad Station] report the enemy is advancing in force on the Leesborough [Wheaton] Road [now Georgia Avenue]. My force is small, but will do my best." He later wired: "The enemy is advancing on my front with cavalry, artillery and infantry." A signal officer later wired: "The enemy is within twenty rods [110 yards] of Fort Stevens."[100]

The *Evening Star* reported in a special third edition of Monday, July 11, that there was "skirmishing between 11 and 12 o'clock on and around the 7th street turnpike, near the Clagett [sic] farm [south of the Blair property west of Georgia Avenue in the District of Columbia], and the residence of Francis P. Blair, Esq. It is reported today [erroneously] that the rebels have burned the residence of Mr. Blair."[101] A July 11 *New York Times* dispatch also said that Postmaster General Montgomery Blair's "Falkland" mansion had been burned by the Rebels. The dispatch was inaccurate when it was written but had been rendered accurate by later events when it was finally received in New York and published three days later. The *Times* also reported that "a resident in the vicinity of Mr. Blair's house, who watched the rebels pass that point, states that they took over an hour to go by. The body consisted exclusively of infantry."[102]

A later report in the *Evening Star* said the Rebel cavalry had arrived near Francis Preston Blair's home and had "kept that position." The paper also noted that there had been "some firing between the pickets; and two or three on our side have been wounded…The rebel force at Silver Spring is said to be about 15,000 strong as so far developed…Preparations have been made to receive them in becoming style."[103]

After returning from Cape May in late July, Elizabeth Blair Lee wrote an account of area residents and the events at "Silver Spring" when the

Confederates occupied it on July 11 and how General Breckinridge had minimized the damage:

> *Bernie* [Martha Barnes, the wife of John T. Barnes, who lived near the "Silver Spring" mansion]…*sent Jim* [Byrnes] *down here for Ned* [Byrnes] *when she heard the Rebs were at Rockville. When he got to Graves' store (Talbot's now)* [in Sligo, on the west side of Georgia Avenue just south of Colesville Road] *he was taken prisoner about 10 o'clock. As they stopped at the spring a shell fell among the trees east of the spring and killed one man and wounded another. They then brought him to the house where there was a perfect saturnalia* [an unrestrained and often licentious celebration] *in progress. One man dressed up in Betty's riding habit, pants and all; another in Father's red (Jessies) velvet wrapper and took a dance. Others came out of the house in Andrew's uniform and clothing and in Father's old coats of all sorts. With one of the demijohns of Naval whisky brought last fall by Father they had a great frolic. Others went on rampaging and robbing until five o'clock when up rode General Early and General Breckinridge. Jim says they were in a great rage with some officer commanding here for stopping here. General Early said "You have ruined our whole campaign. If you had pushed into the Forts this morning at 8 o'clock we could have taken them. Now they have reinforcements from Grant and we can't take them without immense loss; perhaps it is impossible."*
>
> *General Breckinridge began to curse some soldiers with things taken out of the house—the piano cover was used as a horse blanket. He made him give it back, and he put him in irons. He sent for another Regiment to guard the house. General Early said it is "no use to fret about one house when we have lost so much by this proceeding." Then General Breckinridge replied "This place is the only one I felt was a home to me on this side of the Mountains." So Jim took this turn of the talk to let him know this was his home too, and he stepped forward to those Generals and said he lived here and that he would like now to go to his Mother* [at Sligo] *who was alone. John Breckinridge then asked him about all of us, where we were and when we left. When Jim told them, John remarked "that accounts for their leaving everything exposed in this way." He sent Jim home with Blair's donkey.* [Blair was Elizabeth Blair Lee's son, who would celebrate his seventh birthday in less than a month and who became a U.S. senator in 1914.] *Jim asked for it and went to the lane*

and got it, and he started off on it. He had scarce been home [at his mother's] *an hour about midnight when five soldiers stopped and demanded the grey horse and followed Jim where it was hid. And there was poor Jack* [the donkey] *too. He was seized and again carried off. Jim took Old Ned* [her son Blair's dog] *home too, but he slipped his collar and was not to be seen for a week. Jim had been kept here as a prisoner from 10 o'clock in the morning until 9 in the evening.* [104]

Four days after Early reached Silver Spring, the *Evening Star* published an eyewitness account from J.E. Turton, "who enjoyed superior opportunities for observation, having been in the hands of the rebels at Silver Spring during their entire stay there." Turton, who had a contract to remodel Montgomery Blair's house, said that about 11:00 a.m. on Monday morning, six Rebels "dropped down upon him as if from the skies."

They inquired whose house it was, and particularly if it was the house of Lincoln's Postmaster General, and on learning that it was, the leader of the gang exclaimed to the others, "This house must go up!" The house was locked up, (not being in present use by Mr. Blair,) and they proceeded to break open the doors and despoil it, scattering books (of which they seemed to have an indifferent opinion) and papers around in every direction, and carrying off whatever they deemed would be of use to them.

They did the same at the house of Francis P. Blair, and found there what they deemed an especial prize, an excellent county map of the state of Maryland. This map was carefully borne away, and for many hours afterwards a corps of Rebel draughtsmen [sic] *(occupying the house of Thomas Gettings* [a wheelwright whose house was on the east side of Georgia Avenue near today's Fidler Lane, north of Colesville Road] *at the third toll gate) were busily employed over it making sketches and copies. The main body of the Rebel forces did not appear in front of Fort Stevens, but remained encamped on the Wilson farm about a mile and a half beyond Blair's on the 7ᵗʰ street road.* [105]

Turton also said that Early had "not less than 25,000 or 30,000 men" at the Wilson farm and that they also had 576 prisoners taken at Monocacy under guard there. He also said that he spoke to Rebel troops who "talked quite freely of what they would do if they got possession of Washington. They would not leave one stone upon another." The officers were less forthcoming about their intentions. [106]

Richard T. Wilson's home, still standing at 8818 First Avenue, served as headquarters for Confederate major general John C. Breckinridge during Early's raid. Breckinridge and other officers received a friendly welcome, including a banquet prepared by Mrs. Wilson. This photo is of the home's west elevation, which was the front of the house during the Civil War. In the late 1870s, the wings on either side of the porch were added and the front door was moved to the east side of the house, away from the recently opened Metropolitan Branch of the B&O Railroad. *Photo by the author.*

The *National Intelligencer*, quoting the weekly *Washington Chronicle*, also reported on Turton's experience with the Confederates at the "Falkland" mansion:

> *The men were a hard looking, ragamuffin gathering, and were inquisitive on all points, though without using personal violence to Mr. Turton. Many other houses in the neighborhood, both rich and poor, were robbed and ransacked, One other country seat (probably Mr. Belcher's) was also discovered in flames.* [107]

In addition to occupying the Wilson farm, the Confederates also occupied the area to the east as far as Sligo Creek and used Dr. Henry Ford Condict's house (still standing at 9315 Greyrock Road, on the hill west of the creek and north of Colesville Road in Woodside Forest) as an observation post. Two small camps were set up near Dr. Condict's house as a rendezvous point for cavalry searching for horses and other plunder. [108]

Dr. Condict's house, still standing on the hilltop at 9315 Greyrock Road, served as a Confederate observation post. 1998 photo. *Maryland–National Capital Park and Planning Commission.*

News of Early's arrival at Silver Spring, his continuing advance and the refugees ("terror-stricken fugitives," as the *New York Times* called them)[109] fleeing into the city added to the fear already felt by Washingtonians. There was even speculation that Lee was willing to or even planning to, in effect, trade Union capture of Petersburg or Richmond for a Confederate capture of Washington.[110] The fact that Lee had removed troops from the defense of Richmond gave some support to this speculation. Further evidence that Lee was planning a full-fledged onslaught on Washington was claimed to come from the dying words of a Confederate officer captured at the Battle of Monocacy:

> *A rebel Lieutenant, mortally wounded, called, in his faintness, for some water or brandy. Some of the latter was given him, and he then, with great solemnity and conscious of his moribund state, averred that the Confederate force numbered twenty thousand men—that this was but one half of their force, the remaining half having diverged on another road* [indeed, some of Early's troops had moved toward Baltimore], *and that an additional column of forty thousand men under General Lee was on its way up to join the force then in Maryland.*[111]

Adding to nervousness in Washington was the fact that the Rebels had cut both Washington's telegraph connection to the rest of the United States and the rail line to the north. The last operating telegraph line, "the one on the Philadelphia railroad…was cut at 11½ o'clock a.m.," Monday, July 11. To the government and the citizens alike, the city appeared to be under siege and on the verge of capture. The populace didn't learn until the next day that the American Telegraph Company had managed to get one line to the north working again "at a late hour" Monday night.[112]

Early may have chosen to go through Wheaton and Silver Spring on his way to Washington in part because Fort Stevens, just west of Georgia Avenue, was one of the weaker forts north of Washington. It was on less rugged ground and in a somewhat less commanding position than other forts even though it was on the crest of a hill. It also was not especially heavily armed in comparison to some of the other forts. It had four twenty-four-pounder seacoast cannon firing *en barbette* (over the parapet rather than through openings in the fort wall), six twenty-four-pounder siege guns, two eight-inch siege howitzers and five thirty-pound Parrotts firing through openings in the fortification walls. It also had a ten-inch siege and a twenty-four-pounder Coehorn (portable, short-range) mortar and three vacant platforms.[113]

Although the less than truly formidable Fort Stevens was the primary military obstacle directly in the Confederates' path, the extreme weather was also an obstacle. But the heat affected the defenders as well as Early's troops. A Union soldier later recalled his experience on Monday morning when his unit was ordered to go from Fort Stevens to Fort Reno and stationed in rifle pits: "Until one o'clock the grumbling of the men under the intolerable heat in that shadeless plain 'was all the sound we heard.' After resting a few moments, we were ordered back [to Fort Stevens] again. On our arrival one-

Fort Stevens viewed from the north, as the advancing Confederates would have seen it. *Photo by the author.*

Fort Stevens, 1864. *Library of Congress.*

third of the regiment and five commissioned officers had been stricken down with heat and sun-stroke."[114]

As Early's troops began advancing that Monday morning, Fort Stevens was manned by only about two hundred untrained troops, a force that was clearly inadequate in both numbers and experience to stop Early's thousands. One veteran who returned to the fort said he and his fellow veterans had "the mortification of seeing the artillery entrusted to troops who could hardly load heavy ordnance with safety."[115]

Something had to be done, and done quickly. Major General Alexander McDowell McCook later reported:

Monday morning discovered the fact that the only troops on the north of Washington were small garrisons in the forts, small detachments of cavalry in the front, and the troops above mentioned [D.C. volunteers and other units in the rear at Piney Branch]. Hearing of the near approach of the enemy, the idea of a reserve camp was at once abandoned and every man was brought forward and posted in the rifle-pits to the best advantage, and as strong a skirmish line as was prudent established. During the morning several additional regiments of the Veteran Reserve

Corps [i.e., the former Invalid Corps] *and several detachments of dismounted cavalry reported for duty. They were posted in the rifle-pits on either side of the main road leading to Silver Spring.*[116]

McCook also noted that "Captain Berry, of the Eighth Illinois Cavalry, being stationed with his company on the road leading from Silver Spring to Leesborough [now Wheaton], dispatched a courier at 10 a.m. on the 11th, informing me that the enemy was advancing in force on that road with infantry, artillery, and cavalry."[117]

The *Evening Star* reported in its special third edition that "this morning arms were given out to the employees of several of the departments, who have organized for the defense of the city. This afternoon the clerks of the Adjutant General's office were drilling in front of Lafayette Square, fully armed and equipped. A number of the patients in the hospitals, able to bear arms for a short time, have been sent out—about 250 going from Campbell Hospital [a makeshift facility at Florida Avenue and Seventh Street] this morning."[118]

Union major John V. Brinton later recalled, "The Secretary of War directed that all orderlies, messengers, military riffraff, the invalids, veteran reserve, and indeed every man in Government employ who could put on a uniform, or carry a musket, should turn out in defense of the capital of his country." In fact, War Department civilian clerks and about 2,800 injured but recuperating soldiers (the Invalid Corps/Veteran Reserve Corps) were sent to the forts on the north side of Washington. The Invalid Corps/Veteran Reserves wore "sickly" light blue uniforms and were termed "condemned Yankees" by Early's troops.[119] Even the astronomers from the Naval Observatory were called to military duty.[120] Lincoln's personal "Bucktails" guards were sent to the front, as were the few troops guarding the strategic C&O Canal in Montgomery County, who were called back to the city. This led to their blockhouses being burned by Mosby's raiders from across the Potomac, although Mosby did not drain the canal or destroy any locks. The D.C. Militia, under the command of "worthy grocer Brigadier General [Peter F.] Bacon," also issued "General Orders, No. 1," calling out for immediate service lasting thirty days the "Militia and Volunteers of this District." "Every available man is wanted immediately, and captains of companies and colonels of regiments will at once notify the men of their respective commands to assemble for muster without delay."[121]

General Halleck summed up the lack of defenders this way: "We have five times as many generals as we want but are greatly in need of privates. Anyone volunteering in that capacity will be thankfully received."[122]

One of those privates, presumably from the Veteran Reserve Corps or dismounted cavalry, recalled his experience and thankful reception going toward Fort Stevens: "As your correspondent and the sunlight passed up Fourteenth-street, the thunder of the guns at Fort Reno, which were bellowing under the frantic practice of the militia, was swaying the people to and fro with excitement. A broad grin was very hideously perceptible on the secession mouth, and many an anxious face looked out from behind a waving flag, and many a hearty 'God bless you,' came from a loyal heart as we marched up the road."[123]

Not every "loyal heart" had stayed to cheer the troops. As soon as Register of the Treasury L.E. Chittenden heard the estimates of the number of troops in Early's forces Monday morning, he gathered up his family and within two hours was "speeding northward at the rate of forty miles an hour" on the last train that made it to Baltimore. He got off in Baltimore and sent his family on to Philadelphia "out of harms' way."[124]

Early's forces continued their advance toward Fort Stevens as Monday afternoon grew hotter and hotter. They were strung out for miles along Veirs Mill Road and Georgia Avenue. Other Confederate units not with the main body of troops continued to probe throughout southern Montgomery County and into the District, especially down Old Georgetown Road toward Fort Reno and then in the area to the east toward Fort DeRussy, in today's Rock Creek Park.

The Confederate advance was welcomed by at least some Silver Spring residents. Artificer (an enlisted man trained to repair small arms) Nelson A. Fitts of the New York Heavy Artillery, who later escaped after having been taken prisoner by the Confederates on July 10, reported that he had been taken with Early's headquarters unit from Rockville and arrived at Silver Spring about 3:00 p.m. on Monday. "The cavalry joined the rest of the command between Rockville and the Seventh-street road, and I passed the entire length of it; saw their troops and artillery. I also observed some of the inhabitants that gave them information in regard to the forces in Washington." He offered to go back and find these informers.[125]

Early's arrival was also welcomed by some in Washington. According to *Sacramento Union* correspondent Noah Brooks, "In Georgetown one nest of secessionists was rudely broken in upon by the provost guard, who discovered a half-finished Confederate flag in the house. The men were marched over to the guardhouse, and the unfinished colors, probably intended to be presented to Early, were promptly confiscated. This was not the only flag made to be presented to the rebels when they should effect their triumphal entry into Washington."[126]

As the Confederates drew closer to Washington that Monday afternoon, most of the few available Union infantry troops were moved to skirmish lines in front of Fort Stevens. They were told to move around to create the impression that there were more defenders than there really were. They were also ordered not to conserve ammunition but to fire as often as possible at any real or imagined target, again to give the impression that there was a large body of troops defending the forts.[127] Given the number of available troops and their lack of experience and readiness, such bluffing might have been the best defense available.

The Union forces also prepared by clearing out structures in front of Fort Stevens that might give shelter to the Confederates. The *Evening Star* reported that on Monday, several houses along Georgia Avenue were destroyed to keep them from being used as firing points by Rebel sharpshooters. "Among the houses destroyed were Messrs. Richard Butts' [just east of Fort Stevens], Wm. Bell's [just north of the fort], J.H. McChesney's [on the east side of Georgia Avenue at about Tuckerman Street], Mr. [Abner] Shoemakers's [about a mile north of Fort Stevens, more or less at Geranium Street, just east of Georgia Avenue], and the house occupied by the family of the late Wm. M. Morrison. Time, however, was allowed the owners of these to remove the furniture, and the road leading to this city was lined with wagons conveying it to a place of safety."[128]

The *Evening Star* also reported, "The farmers in the vicinity lost most of their stock, owing, as they say, to our pickets refusing to let the drivers pass through the lines without a permit. The farmers had taken the precaution to drive their stock towards the city as the rebels advanced but, not being allowed to enter, it fell into the hands of the enemy."[129]

Around 1:30 p.m. on Monday, the sound of artillery fire from the north notified Washington residents that the Confederates were at their doorstep.[130] Early later recalled that as his troops arrived near Fort Stevens, "[Colonel George H.] Smith drove a small body of cavalry before him into the woods on the 7th Street pike, and dismounted his men and deployed them as skirmishers. I rode ahead of the infantry, and arrived in sight of Fort Stevens on the road a short time after noon, when I discovered that the works were but feebly manned."[131]

He ordered Major General Robert Rodes' division, which was in front but spread out along the road, to get in line, send out skirmishers and take the fort if it could. But before the troops could get into line, he saw "a cloud of

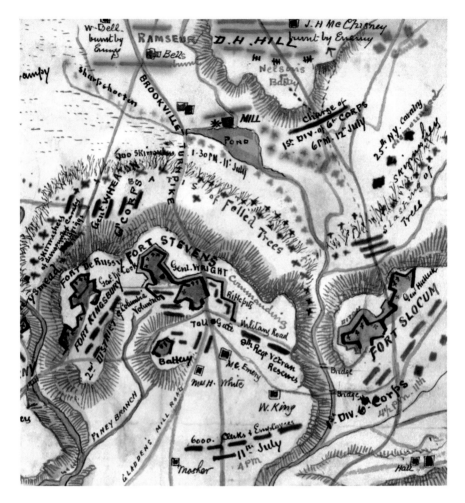

Detail from the plan of the Rebel attack on Washington, D.C., July 11 and 12, 1864. Copy of official plan made in the office of Colonel Alexander, USA, chief engineer of the defense of Washington, September 1864. This map severely compresses the area between Fort Reno and Fort Stevens and erroneously places Fort DeRussy and Battery Kingsbury east of Rock Creek. They were actually west of the creek and northeast of Fort Kearny. *Library of Congress.*

dust in the rear of the works towards Washington, and soon a column of the enemy filed into them on the right and left and skirmishers were thrown out in front, while an artillery fire was opened on us from a number of batteries. This defeated our hopes of getting possession of the works by surprise, and it became necessary to reconnoitre [*sic*]."[132]

Rodes' skirmishers were thrown to the front, driving those of the enemy to the cover of the works, and we proceeded to examine the fortifications in order to ascertain if it was practicable to carry them by assault. They were found to be exceedingly strong, and consisted of what appeared to be enclosed forts of heavy artillery, with a tier of lower works in front of each pierced for an immense number of guns, the whole being connected by curtains with ditches in front, and strengthened by palisades and abattis [obstacles made of cut trees and bushes]. *The timber had been felled within cannon range all around and left on the ground, making a formidable obstacle, and every possible approach was raked by artillery. On the right was Rock Creek running through a deep ravine which had been rendered impassable by the felling of the timber on each side, and beyond were the works on the Georgetown pike* [Fort Reno] *which had been reported to be the strongest of all. On the left, as far as the eye could reach, the works appeared to be of the same impregnable character. The position was naturally strong for defence* [sic], *and the examination showed, what might have been expected, that every appliance of science and unlimited means had been used to render the fortifications around Washington as strong as possible. This reconnaissance consumed the balance of the day.*[133]

Early also noted that the long march up the valley and through Maryland had greatly diminished his forces. He estimated that only a third of his infantry troops "could have been carried into action" and that he only "had about forty pieces of field artillery, of which the largest were 12 pounder Napoleons, besides a few pieces of horse artillery with the cavalry." He went on to say:

McCausland reported the works on the Georgetown pike too strongly manned for him to assault. We could not move to the right or left without its being discovered from a signal station on the top of the "Soldiers' Home," which overlooked the country, and the enemy would have been enabled to move in his works to meet us. Under the circumstances, to have rushed my men blindly against the fortifications, without understanding the state of things, would have been worse than folly. If we had any friends in Washington, none of them came out to give us information, and this satisfied me that the place was not undefended. I knew that troops had arrived from Grant's army, for prisoners had been captured from Rickett's division of the 6th corps at Monocacy.[134]

Fort Reno Signal Tower. Another signal station was at the Soldiers' Home. *Library of Congress.*

"Brisk skirmishing" broke out in front of Fort Stevens. Confederate sharpshooters, using an orchard and houses not already destroyed by Union defenders for cover, managed to advance to "within 30 or 40 rods"[135] or perhaps even 20 rods (little more than the length of a football field) of the fort.[136] The ferocity of the skirmish convinced Early that his forces, tired and still strung out along the roads from Rockville, could not succeed in an immediate attack, especially when he saw veteran reinforcements arriving and forming a skirmish line.[137] In 1881, he recalled, "The whole command had then marched fully fifteen miles in very hot, dry weather and over exceedingly dusty roads, and was, of course, very much exhausted, many of the men having fallen by the way from heat and sheer exhaustion."[138] Nevertheless, had he pressed the attack on Monday afternoon, he might well have overwhelmed Fort Stevens from force of numbers alone despite the condition of his own army. Or he might have bypassed the fort.

At least that is what Confederate general John B. Gordon thought:

> *I myself rode to a point on* [the Union outer defensive works] *at which there was no force whatever. The unprotected space was broad enough for easy passage of Early's army without resistance. It is true that as we approached, Rodes's division had driven in some skirmishers, and during the day (July 11th) another small affair had occurred on the Seventh Street road; but all the Federals encountered on this approach could not have manned any considerable portion of the defences. Undoubtedly we could have marched into Washington.*
>
> *In a council of war called by General Early there was not a dissenting opinion as to the impolicy of entering the city. While General Early and his division commanders were considering in jocular vein the propriety of putting* [former U.S. vice president and now Early's second in command] *General John C. Breckinridge at the head of a column and escorting him to the Senate chamber and seating him again in the Vice-President's chair, the sore-footed men in gray were lazily lounging about the cool waters of Silver Spring, picking blackberries in the orchards of Postmaster-General Blair, and merrily estimating the amount of gold and greenbacks that would come into our possession when we should seize the vaults of the United States Treasury.*[139]

General Gordon went on to say that he thought ordinary soldiers did not really expect to go into the city.[140]

Early later justified his failure to attack the fort immediately this way:

> *The idea…that I could have entered Washington by a vigorous assault on the works on my arrival is without any well-grounded foundation. It took several hours to bring my infantry into line, as it was moving by flank on*

a narrow road, with the trains and artillery interspersed at intervals on the line of march for the purposes of protection, one division being in rear of the whole. Before even the first brigade of the leading division was brought into line, I saw a cloud of dust from the direction of Washington, showing that troops were moving up, and a portion of them having filed into the trenches, a large body of skirmishers was sent to the front, which drove back my cavalry skirmishers, about two hundred strong, and burned a number of houses in front of the works.

He also noted:

My artillery did not exceed forty field pieces, manned by six or seven hundred men, and they would have been of no use to me in an attack, for there were so many of the enemy's guns bearing upon every position within range, and they were so much heavier metal, that I would not have been able to put one of mine in position, and I made no attempt to do so; consequently, not a piece of my artillery was fired in front of Washington.[141]

Although he didn't mount a full-scale attack that afternoon, Early continued harassing the defenders and keeping his options open. Confederate sharpshooters in an orchard north of Fort Stevens were particularly effective. For a while, they managed to drive the fort's artillery crews from their guns. At one point during the afternoon, Union defenders seized a privately owned buggy to rush bullets to soldiers who were running out of ammunition in a skirmish line in front of Fort Stevens.[142]

Around noon, Lincoln, who had gone out to see the defenses at Tenleytown, Fort Reno and Fort Stevens earlier in the morning, greeted the first reinforcements from the Sixth Corps arriving at the Sixth Street wharfs. As the day went on, additional veteran troops arrived at the wharves from the Richmond area, refreshed by the boat trip. One colonel noted, "To enjoy a cool breeze without blinding dust is a luxury we have not been accustomed to for months."[143] Once off the boats after some confusion—the arriving troops (two divisions of the Sixth Corps) were originally marched up Pennsylvania Avenue past the Treasury and White House on their way to Chain Bridge—the troops were redirected up Eleventh Street and then toward Fort Stevens. One officer recalled:

The sight of the Veterans of the Sixth Corps was an immense relief to the constitutionally timid Washingtonians. We passed through crowded streets;

cheers, good wishes, and fervent God-speeds were heard on every side. Citizens ran through the lines with buckets of ice-water, for the morning was sultry; newspapers and eatables were handed into the column, and our welcome had a heartiness that showed how intense had been the fear.[144]

The remainder of the reinforcements sent from City Point, the rest of the Sixth Corps and the Nineteenth Corps, subsequently arrived at the wharfs. The first group eventually got to Crystal Spring, near Fort Stevens, around 4:00 p.m. The strategy was to hold the veterans in reserve so they could quickly be sent to wherever Early decided to attack.[145]

Skirmishing between the first arrivals from Early's forces and the few Union defenders had broken out at Fort Stevens while Lincoln was there, so he undoubtedly was very happy to see the veteran troops arrive. So was an enthusiastic crowd of local residents.

Lieutenant Colonel Thomas W. Hyde described the scene at Fort Stevens this way:

By noon we reached the line of works at Fort Stevens and found a rattled lot of defenders, brave enough, but with no coherence or organization. Within the forts there were plenty of brigadier-generals with new shoulder straps wandering proudly about, the treasury guards pale with anticipated battle, the quartermasters and commissary men, reserve batteries, all war's motley; and without, as fine a corps of infantry as ever marched to tap the drum were closing in upon the capitol, with the stars and bars waving.[146]

A Union soldier described what Lincoln saw and heard:

By two o'clock the rebel skirmishers were appearing and disappearing, in that snake-in-the-grass style so becoming to their status, near the residence of Hon. FRANK BLAIR. By three o'clock their skirmish line had worked its insidious way within pistol shot of the gunners at the fort, and matters were becoming decidedly interesting, sufficiently so to beguile the President, the Secretary of State [Seward] and his son, many of the foreign Legations, and all the military notabilities of the capital, to the scene.

So close were they that one of the gazers from Fort Stevens was shot on the parapet, and the whistle of a bullet was heard close beside the President's carriage, which, at this stage of the proceedings, was in a position enabling its distinguished occupant to crack a joke in response to the crack of the rebel rifle.

Whether it was this last outrage that determined the officers in charge or not we do not know; but about this time proceedings were being taken to put an end to this rebel recreation.

A line of skirmishers, composed of the Veteran Reserves, some dismounted cavalry and hundred-day men, were deployed in front, and steadily drove back for a short distance the whole rebel line.

The scene at this time was one of the rarest in history. From the elevated position of the intrenchments [sic] *the view was unobstructed for ten miles in every direction but a few groans* [sic] *of trees and underbrush. This beautiful agricultural region under the guns of Fort Stevens and De Russey* [sic] *was radiant with the glory of the ripening harvest, and the splendor of unclouded sunlight. Light puffs of smoke shot out from the dark-green*

John C. Breckinridge, Confederate major general, former U.S. vice president, 1860 presidential candidate and friend and relative of the Blairs. *Library of Congress.*

verdure and great white wreaths from the bursting shells circled against the deep blue sky. From the burning dwelling, which our skirmishers were destroying, in order to give range to the artillery, secession families were pouring through the lines, with deep and audible curses, uttered within reach of the Presidential ear, and loyal families, with sorrow-stricken faces, were hurrying toward the city.

A vast audience with hushed voices and earnest gaze were looking out upon the scene, and there, insight of the greatest men of the day, with honest ABRAHAM *on one side of the rifle-pits and dishonest* JOHN C. BRECKINRIDGE *on the other. The Postmaster-General saw his house, the headquarters of his former friend, and now traitor enemy, who was struggling to destroy the very capital where the people had delighted to do him honor.* [The soldier was in error about the presence of Postmaster General Montgomery Blair.]

This was the last scene your correspondent's eyes rested upon as he went over the breastwork to get a nearer view in obedience to the order, "In Advance March" of his officer.[147]

Additional reinforcements (the first six hundred troops of the Nineteenth Corps) arrived at the docks from New Orleans during the afternoon and evening. They were sent out the Bladensburg Road to guard the eastern approach to the city, where more Confederates were feared approaching.

At about 3:00 p.m., Major General Horatio G. Wright, the commander of the Sixth Corps, arrived at Fort Stevens and said his men would be arriving shortly thereafter. He was ordered to send nine hundred of his veteran troops out for picket duty during the night.

By about 5:00 p.m., Early's line had gotten as close as about one hundred yards from Fort Stevens, but by sundown (around 7:20 p.m. on July 11 in Washington before the introduction of time zones and daylight saving time), they had been driven back by Union defenders, some of whom had arrived only recently, and by artillery fire from Fort DeRussy to the west and Forts Slocum and Totten to the east.

Fort DeRussy from the north, as the Confederates would have seen it. The woods of today's Rock Creek Park were cleared at the time of the battle. *Photo by the author.*

Fort Totten. *Library of Congress.*

The forts also fired longer-range shots to harass the Confederates as they advanced down Georgia Avenue toward and beyond Silver Spring. Fort DeRussy's one-hundred-pounder Parrott gun lobbed shells over two and a half miles into what is now the Woodside Park neighborhood.

John H. Worsham, a Confederate soldier, remembered his march down Georgia Avenue and the Union defenses this way:

We were up and moving early the next morning [Monday, July 11], *passing through Rockville, Maryland, and at two or three P.M. the head of Gordon's division passed the toll gate about four or five miles from Washington* [the tollgate just south of where Colesville Road now intersects Georgia Avenue]. *We inquired what road we were on, and were informed that it was the Seventh Street pike. The enemy were shelling the road at this point with their big guns. We soon came in sight of the Soldiers' Home, where the enemy had a signal station, and we were really at Washington City. We could see their fortifications and the men marching into them on each side of the road on which we were. Their dress induced us to think they were the town or city forces, some of them looking as if they had on linen dusters, and there being none in regular uniform.*

Probably the day was hotter than the preceding, and we had been marching faster too. Consequently there was more straggling. Our division was stretched out almost like skirmishers, and all the men did not get up until night. Rodes' division was in front. He had formed a line of battle and sent forward his skirmishers, who had driven the enemy into their fortifications. Our division stacked arms on the side of the road, the men broke ranks and looked around. A house between the two lines was burning. I went to Silver Springs [sic], *the country home of Mr. Blair, one of Lincoln's cabinet* [the home was actually Francis Preston Blair's "Silver Spring," not the home of cabinet member Montgomery Blair], *and got water, and examined the place. It was a splendid home. When I came back I went to the front and looked out on the situation. As far as my eye could reach to the right and left there were fortifications, and the most formidable looking I ever saw! In their front the trees had been cut down so that the limbs pointed towards us and they were sharpened. About midway of the clearing was a creek that seemed to run near the fortifications and parallel with them. The enemy had a full sweep of the ground for at least a mile in their front, and if their works were well manned, our force would not be able to take them, since, as I suppose, Gen. Early's entire command did not number 10,000. Night came on and found us occupying the same position.*[148]

By nightfall, the Union defenders had established a two-mile line extending from in front of Fort DeRussy on the west to in front of Fort Slocum to the east. In front of Fort Stevens, the line was slightly south of today's intersection of Piney Branch Road and Georgia Avenue. The Confederate skirmish line was about a quarter of a mile farther north near what later was the Walter Reed Army Medical Center campus before the hospital's 2011 consolidation with the National Naval Medical Center in Bethesda.

General Early set up his headquarters at Francis Preston Blair's temporarily vacated "Silver Spring" mansion. The Confederates were reported also to have set up a field hospital there and "were seen to carry some of their wounded into it."[149] Indeed, the *National Intelligencer* reported that about one hundred Confederate wounded were left there when Early retreated.[150] Early, however, later stated that Blair's mansion was not used as a hospital, saying, "If any wounded men were found in it they were men who had been wounded in the affair which occurred late in the afternoon of the 12th [Tuesday] between some troops sent out from the works [Fort Stevens] and a portion of the troops on my front line, who would not be transported and found their way to the house after I retired."[151] The Confederate field hospital tents were set up at the Sligo Post Office (depicted after the Confederates left in the 1937 Silver Spring Post Office mural now at the Silver Spring Library) near the third tollgate, just below where Colesville Road from the northeast ended at Georgia Avenue.[152]

Shelling forced troops camping in the open fields of the Wilson farm to withdraw to the safety of the woods north of the present Highland Drive. "Very heavy bodies" of Confederate infantry bivouacked along Georgia Avenue north as far as William Batchelor's farm (east of Georgia Avenue, on the north side of Forest Glen Road). Other reports say some of Early's forces were also camped in the Wheaton area.

Colonel John M.C. Marble, who was ordered to take charge of Fort DeRussy on Monday, July 11, filed a somewhat less than modest post-battle report on July 16, stating:

Noticing a considerable movement of the enemy in the vicinity of Wilson's house, on the Seventh Street Road [just north of Spring Street on the east side of what is now Georgia Avenue], *we deemed it advisable to send in a few shells. We are assured by citizens in that direction that the enemy was surprised at the accuracy of our fire at such a distance, and from information since obtained we are led to conclude that the accuracy and activity of our artillery and skirmish line contributed to deter them from making the intended assault on Monday night.*[153]

After Early's retreat, the chief of artillery at Fort DeRussy, Captain John Norris of the Second Provisional Pennsylvania Heavy Artillery, rode out and surveyed the area to see what damage the thirty-two shots of his one-hundred-pounder Parrott gun had done. He filed a report stating:

We fired 18 case-shot, 10 shells, and 4 solid shot. Twenty-two of these were fired on Monday evening and Tuesday morning on column of enemy moving down the Brookeville turnpike [Georgia Avenue] *toward*

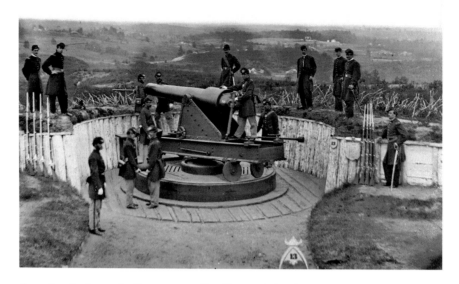

A one-hundred-pounder Parrott gun at Fort Totten; similar Parrott guns were also used at Fort DeRussy. *Library of Congress.*

Fort Stevens, and at trains parked in the fields adjoining the turnpike, as a distance, as near as I could estimate, of from 4,200 to 4,500 yards [roughly two and a half miles]. *Elevation and length of fuse were given for these distances. Having the use of a powerful glass, I considered the shots effective, at least in causing the enemy to move their trains and troops from time to time, and yesterday, as I made a close inspection of that point, found the enemy had been there in force. Two shells had exploded and struck the outbuildings of Mr. John Wilson, just to the right of the turnpike, about half a mile beyond Silver Spring; one had entered the ground a half mile farther to the north* [near the intersection of Alton and Woodside Parkways] *and exploded; others exploded just this side* [west] *of the turnpike, and as I learned from a citizen resident near by, caused at least a division of the enemy to transfer their camp to a woods beyond.*[154]

Norris went on to report that they had also fired eight spherical case shots from their thirty-two-pounder seacoast gun that exploded in the air above a line of Confederate skirmishers about a mile from Fort DeRussy. They later found "the carcass of a fine stallion killed by one of our shells" and concluded from the location of the horse's wound that his rider had also been severely wounded. "The body of one rebel was found at a distance of

A trail leading into the remnants of Fort DeRussy. There were no trees in 1864. *Photo by the author.*

2,600 yards [slightly less than a mile and a half] in the direction of our firing badly mutilated by a piece of shell, and I am informed that a number of the severely wounded left at Silver Spring were wounded by our shells."[155]

A Confederate soldier described the shelling this way: "When we were approaching the city and were still some miles away, those who occupied the defenses opened on us with siege guns of heavy caliber. As these monster shells passed over our heads and the tops of the trees they made a roaring noise like the passing of a railroad train, but they burst far to the rear and did no harm. We knew from this that they were fired by inexperienced gunners. Someone remarked facetiously that perhaps they were shelling our wagon train."[156]

He also noted that "the report of [the Confederates' heaviest artillery] in comparison with that of the heavy guns of the [defenders] was like that of popguns in the hands of schoolboys."[157]

Chapter 8

PREPARATIONS FOR ATTACK

Monday Night, July 11–12, 1864

On Monday evening, General Early conferred with the senior officers under his command—and drank from Francis Preston Blair's wine cellar with his officers. He was concerned that he had to attack quickly if he was to attack Washington at all. He had read in a Northern newspaper that Union general Hunter had come up the Ohio River and was on his way by rail to Harpers Ferry. He feared Hunter's forces would cut off his escape route over South Mountain and fords on the upper Potomac. "Being very reluctant to abandon the project of capturing Washington, I determined to make an assault on the enemy's works at daylight next morning [Tuesday, July 12], unless some information should be received before that time showing its impracticability."[158]

Union reinforcements arrived during the late evening and night. At about 9:00 p.m., Quartermaster General Montgomery Meigs reported to Fort Stevens with 1,500 armed and equipped quartermaster employees. They were sent to man rifle pits on either side of Fort Slocum. There was fear that Early was planning to attack to the right of Fort Stevens. Fort Slocum was on the right between Fort Stevens and Fort Totten. At about 10:00 p.m., about 2,800 "convalescents and men from the hospitals" arrived. They were sent to a position at the rear of Fort Slocum.

Reinforcements weren't the only people going to Fort Stevens. According to the *Evening Star*, "Early in the evening thousands of persons could be seen passing out Seventh street by every conceivable means of conveyance, while the road was literally lined with pedestrians. The hills, trees, and fences within sight of Fort Stevens were covered with human beings, quite a number of whom were ladies. Quietly seated in a carriage at a commanding point was Secretary [of State] Seward viewing the progress of affairs."[159]

Navy secretary Welles was among the many who had gone to Fort Stevens on Monday. He wanted to see what was going on and find out where the Confederates were. He more or less correctly, as it turned out, summed up the situation and expressed his frustration in his diary Monday evening, saying that nobody really knew the disposition of the Confederate forces and that they could only tell him the Confederates were

> *over the hills, pointing in the direction of Silver Spring...Are they near Gunpowder [River, northeast of Baltimore] or Baltimore? Where are they? Oh! Within a short distance, a mile or two only. I asked why their whereabouts was not ascertained, and their strength known. The reply was that we had no fresh cavalry.*
>
> *The truth is the forts around Washington have been vacated and the troops sent to General Grant, who was promised reinforcements to take Richmond. But he has been in its vicinity more than a month, resting, apparently, after his bloody march, but has effected nothing since his arrival on the James [River], nor displayed any strategy, while Lee has sent a force threatening the National Capital, and we are without force for its defense. Citizens are volunteering, and the employees in the navy yard are required to man the fortifications left destitute...*
>
> *I am sorry to see so little reliable intelligence. It strikes me that the whole demonstration is weak in numbers but strong in conception, that the Rebels have but a small force. I am satisfied no attack is now to be apprehended on the city; the Rebels have lost a remarkable opportunity. But on our part there is neglect, ignorance, folly, imbecility, in the last degree. The Rebels are making a show of fight while they are stealing horses, cattle, etc., through Maryland, They might have easily captured Washington. Stanton, Halleck, and Grant are asleep or dumb.*[160]

At about 10:00 p.m., according to the *National Intelligencer*, "while the Federals were forming their picket line out the Seventh street road near Widow Carberry's [approximately Twelfth and Butternut Streets, NW, on the later Walter Reed Army Medical Center grounds], the Confederates assaulted them with some impetuosity, and drove them back, but the line was finally formed after a slight brush. After this quietness reigned supreme all night."[161]

Troops on both sides spent an uncomfortable night, with occasional firing and general commotion keeping them awake. The Confederates camped in the Woodside and Woodside Park areas were particularly bothered by periodic shelling of their camps by artillery at Fort DeRussy and the other forts.

Register of the Treasury Chittenden, who had gone north with his family earlier in the day, also spent an uncomfortable night—at the Fountain Hotel in Baltimore. He awoke at dawn and "went to the crowded station, and took the first train for Washington. I was the only passenger. At the way stations and road crossings the mounted Confederates were numerous, but as we were running into the city, which they regarded as already virtually in their hands, we were not molested." When he got to Washington, he heard cheering coming from the direction of the corner of Pennsylvania Avenue and Seventh Street.[162] The cheering was for more newly arrived troops.

Chapter 9

SKIRMISHES

Tuesday, July 12, 1864

B y Tuesday morning, the city and Fort Stevens were much better defended than they had been when Early's troops arrived on Monday. Nevertheless, Washington's residents continued to be alarmed about their fate. The fact that refugees from the area north of Fort Stevens were coming down Georgia Avenue with whatever household goods they had managed to salvage from their damaged, destroyed or occupied houses added to the alarm. At least five houses had already been destroyed.[163]

Refugees living outside the Union lines were allowed to pass through the pickets but were not permitted to return to their homes. Union pickets reported that other "small bodies of citizens [were] moving about outside the pickets, claiming to be searching places of refuge, alarmed by the movements of our own and rebel scouting parties."[164] A *Constitutional Union* reporter on his way to Fort Stevens noted, "Just outside the City [i.e., just beyond Florida Avenue] we met several farmers with their teams, hauling into town their household furniture—their dwellings having been destroyed, or taken possession of by the Confederates."[165]

The loyalty of the refugees coming into Washington was open to question. A Union officer who had "explored the adjoining country thoroughly" the previous year "seeking pasturage for horses and mules for the Washington depot" reflected the general suspicion of the refugees, saying that "a large proportion of the men only want opportunity and persuasion to take up arms against the United States."[166]

Public concern was further heightened by rumors and erroneous published reports that Early's army wasn't the only one they had to worry about. The *Constitutional Union* reported a rumor that thirty thousand Rebels under Longstreet were at "Falls Church village." The *Evening Star* and *National Intelligencer* said six to eight hundred Rebels occupied Falls Church.[167] The *New York Times* reported that on Tuesday, July 12, a Union scout had informed Secretary of War Stanton that Monday night he had slept in the camp of Confederate general Longstreet near Manassas Junction, only about thirty miles west of Washington.[168] Actually, Longstreet was recuperating in Augusta, Georgia, from a severe friendly fire wound he had received at the Battle of the Wilderness in May, but according to the *Times*, he was bringing up reinforcements for Early from Gordonsville, which was at the junction of the Orange and Alexandria Railroad with the Central Virginia Railroad (in Orange County, between Charlottesville and Fredericksburg). The Central Virginia Railroad ran from Richmond to Staunton and was reported to have recently been repaired and reopened. Thus, even more Confederate reinforcements could quickly be brought up by rail from the Richmond area to open a second front on the west side of the city.

There were also reports that the telegraph and rail connection to Baltimore had been cut when the Rebels tore up tracks between Beltsville and Laurel and destroyed the Paint Branch and Laurel bridges.[169] In addition, contrabands fleeing into the city from the east said that Confederate cavalry was operating between Beltsville and Bladensburg, which, in fact, it was. The city appeared to be under threat from every direction except the south.

Panic had spread as far as Annapolis, where the *New York Times* reported that "the excitement was intense, rumors having spread like wildfire that the enemy was approaching with the intention of burning the State Capitol. The rebel sympathizers asserted that their idols would not do such an act, as the Jefferson Davis government had too much respect for the building in which Washington resigned his commission. The loyal men of the city did not give them credit for any such good feelings and made preparations to resist any attack. Breastworks were thrown up and rifle-pits dug at the north end of the town." These rumors were actually less ominous than the rumors that had circulated the previous morning, which said the Rebels had taken over Annapolis. A number of people supposedly on their way to join the invading Confederates were arrested.[170]

Rumors of a different sort circulated in Richmond. Supposedly, Rebel troops "with the aid of 15,000 Maryland Secessionists" had captured Baltimore, Fort Stevens had fallen and Early's army had taken Washington at about 10:00 p.m. Monday night. All of the Union's military stores and supplies in Alexandria and all the supplies and public documents in Washington were being taken away by the victorious invaders, according to these reports.[171]

Despite the rumors in Annapolis and Richmond, Early knew it was not to be. During the night, he received a dispatch from Brigadier General Bradley Johnson, who was near Baltimore, informing him that two corps had arrived from General Grant's army and speculating that Grant's whole army was on the way. "This caused me to delay the attack until I could examine the works again, and, as soon as it was light enough to see [about 4:00 a.m.], I rode to the front and found the parapets lined with troops. I had, therefore, reluctantly to give up all hopes of capturing Washington, after I had arrived in sight of the dome of the Capitol and given the Federal authorities a terrible fright."[172]

Early called off the attack. He lacked confidence in his cavalry and didn't believe his artillery could have adequately silenced the Union's much heavier artillery at Forts DeRussy, Stevens, Slocum and Totten. Later, he told Robert E. Lee that he was certain his whole army would have been destroyed if he had attacked, even if he had initially been successful in taking Fort Stevens. Instead of ordering an attack, Early ordered skirmishing, sharpshooting and occasional artillery fire throughout the day.

The Confederates first "appeared in good force" between Fort Stevens and Fort DeRussy "near widow Carberry's woods" (approximately Sixteenth and Geranium Streets, on high ground, near Rock Creek, between Claggett's place and Fort DeRussy). John Worsham, a Confederate soldier, remembered that Gordon's division "marched to the front, formed line of battle, advanced to the edge of the wood and lay down." His own skirmish line "was sent forward to the creek. We remained in our position all day. The enemy were shelling us at intervals, and in the afternoon they sent forward their skirmishers with a large force following them. They made an attack on Rodes' front. He repulsed them and drove them back into their works."[173]

The *Evening Star* reported that "along the entire front line this morning the rebels present a much bolder front than they did yesterday, and the indications are that they have been heavily reinforced by infantry…Our skirmishers now occupy a corn field, while those of the enemy occupy an apple orchard not over a hundred yards distant, and they are continually popping at each other, the rebs however, being careful not to come from under cover."[174] The Union troops dug in to reinforce the gaps between the forts. The *Evening Star* reported that "a large number of contrabands were

"Scene of the Fight in Front of Fort Stevens, July 12 & 13.—From a Sketch by Our Special Artist, E.F. Mullen." *Frank Leslie's Illustrated Newspaper* 18, no. 462 (August 6, 1864), 317. *Library of Congress.*

set to work this morning throwing up fresh rifle pits between the forts. This saves the men from the scorching heat."[175] No doubt it also saved the troops from the Rebel sharpshooters. There was no report as to whether any of the escaped slaves pressed into this service were killed or wounded.

The *Constitutional Union* said:

> *Up to 11 o'clock the skirmishing was continued, the Confederates still endeavoring to reach the field of low bushes on the right of the Seventh street road. At one time they broke cover, and the Federal troops could be seen rushing across the road as though in pursuit. Soon a vigorous banging took place. Several Federals were seen to fall on the right of the road, among them was Col. [John F.] Ballier, of the 98th Pennsylvania, who was shot through the right thigh. The wound is very painful, but not dangerous. All this skirmishing took place within three hundred yards of Fort Stevens, the Confederates occupying the house of widow Carberry.*[176]

The *Evening Star* also reported that there had been considerable skirmishing near Forts Stevens and DeRussy, with the Rebels getting to within three hundred yards of the forts before they were driven back. "Subsequently the rebels appeared in Carberry's woods. They showed themselves here in squads of fifteen and twenty, but a well aimed fire of shells from Forts Stevens and De Russey [*sic*] caused them to get speedily under cover, and afterwards they showed more caution in exposing themselves to view…One of these shells was seen to explode amidst a group of rebels as it fell, doing great execution." Nineteen wounded soldiers were taken down Piney Branch Road in ambulances to hospitals in the city.[177]

At midday, Assistant Secretary of War Charles A. Dana telegraphed a status report to Grant. He reported that there had been "no attack on this city or Baltimore" and that "General McCook has been firing artillery all night from Forts Reno and Massachusetts [Stevens], which remain in his command." The frustrated Dana didn't explicitly say so, but apparently he and Secretary of War Stanton thought it was a very good thing there had been no major attack by the Confederates given the state of the Union leadership, or the lack thereof:

> *Nothing can possibly be done here toward pursuing or cutting off the enemy for want of a commander. General Auger commands the defenses of Washington, with McCook and lot of brigadier-generals under him, but he is not allowed to go outside. Wright commands his own corps.*

[Major] General [Quincy A.] Gillmore has been assigned to the temporary command of those troops of the Nineteenth Corps in the city of Washington. General [Edward O.C.] Ord is to command the Eighth Corps and all other troops in the Middle Department, leaving Wallace to command the city [Baltimore] alone. But there is no head to the whole, and it seems indispensable that you should appoint one. Hunter will be the ranking officer if he ever gets up, but he will not do. Indeed the Secretary of War directs me to tell you in his judgment Hunter ought instantly be relieved, having proven himself far more incompetent than even Sigel. He also directs me to say that advice or suggestions from you will not be sufficient. General Halleck will not give orders except as he receives them; the President will give none, and until you direct positively and explicitly what is to be done, everything will go on in the deplorable and fatal way in which it has gone on for the past week.[178]

Also at midday, Lincoln held his regularly scheduled cabinet meeting, but it was poorly attended. Montgomery Blair, however, had returned from his Pennsylvania outing and did attend, along with Secretary of the Navy Gideon Welles. Welles noted in his diary that Lincoln said that he and Seward had visited several of the forts and that he thought most of the Rebels were at Silver Spring. Welles said he doubted "whether there was any large force at any one point, but that they were in squads of from 500 to perhaps 1500 scattered along from the Gunpowder [River, northeast of Baltimore] to the falls of the Potomac, who kept up an alarm on the outer rim while the marauders were driving off horses and cattle." Lincoln responded that he "thought there must be a pretty large force in the neighborhood of Silver Spring." Welles went on to note in his diary that in discussions with Secretary of War Stanton, "I can obtain no facts, no opinions. He seems dull and stupefied. Others tell me the same."[179]

That afternoon, Welles went to Fort Stevens, where he met Senator Benjamin Franklin Wade of Ohio. They talked a while and concluded there were fewer Confederates facing the fort than there had been the day before. When they went into the fort, they found Lincoln "sitting in the shade, his back against the parapet towards the enemy." The battery soon started shelling the Rebel pickets. That was followed by an assault by two regiments that had been "lying in wait in the valley."[180]

The firing from the battery was accurate. The shells that were sent into a fine mansion occupied by the Rebel sharpshooters soon set it on fire. As the firing from the fort ceased, our men ran to the charge and the Rebels fled. We could see them running across the fields, seeking the woods on the brow of the opposite hills [probably north of Alaska Avenue and the later Walter Reed Army Medical Center grounds]. *It was an interesting and exciting spectacle. But below we could see here and there some of our men bearing away their wounded comrades. I should judge the distance to be something over 300 yards. Occasionally a bullet from some long-range rifle passed above our heads. One man had been shot in the fort a few minutes before we entered.*

As we came out of the fort, four or five of the wounded men were carried by on stretchers. It was nearly dark as we left. Driving in, as was the case when driving out, we passed fields as well as roads full of soldiers, horses, teams, mules. Camp-fires lighted up the woods, which seemed to be more eagerly sought than the open fields.

The day has been exceedingly warm, and the stragglers by the wayside were many. Some were doubtless sick, some were drunk, some were weary and exhausted. The men on horseback, on mules, in wagons as well as on foot, batteries of artillery, caissons, an innumerable throng. It was exciting and wild. Much of life and much of sadness. Strange that in this age and country there is this strife and struggle, under one of the most beneficent governments which ever blessed mankind and all in sight of the Capitol.

In times gone by I had passed over these roads little anticipating scenes like this, and a few years hence they will scarcely be believed to have occurred.[181]

The skirmishing continued into the afternoon. The Rebels next appeared east of Fort Stevens toward Fort Slocum. The Union defenders answered with infantry and artillery. Artillery fire throughout the day from Fort DeRussy (109 shells), Fort Stevens (67 shells) and Fort Slocum (53 shells) targeted houses, farm structures and groves of trees being used by Confederate sharpshooters. Most of these targets were a half mile to a mile from the forts. The Reeves house (about a block east of Georgia Avenue at Butternut Street) was repeatedly hit, scattering the Confederate sharpshooters who were using it. One of the sharpshooters who had been at the top of an oak tree in the front yard fell mortally wounded into lower branches, where his body remained for several days.[182] Union gunners also fired at Early's headquarters at Francis Preston Blair's "Silver Spring" about 1.8 miles from the artillery positions and at Confederate positions farther out in or near Woodside Park. The *Constitutional Union* reported that afternoon that "off in

A house north of Fort Stevens, possibly the Wilkins house, showing effects of the shelling. *Library of Congress.*

the distance [from its reporter's vantage point next to Fort Stevens], out the Seventh Street road, at least three miles [i.e., at about Forest Glen Road], a heavy black smoke was observed as though a dwelling was on fire. It was too much smoke for a camp fire."[183]

Meanwhile, Union squadrons from the Fort Reno area moved up River Road and Rockville Pike to push back Confederate units in that area, and sailors and civilians from the navy yard went to Fort Lincoln to guard the city where the road and railroad from Baltimore entered the District of Columbia. The sailors and navy yard civilians, like most of the ad hoc forces mustered to defend the city, apparently were not well prepared for deployment. In the early hours of the morning on July 13, the rear admiral in charge of them requested that Chief of Staff major general Halleck immediately send him five hundred cups and spoons. Halleck replied some hours later that "cups and spoons are not furnished by the Government to troops."[184]

The Confederate troops had not been told Tuesday morning that they wouldn't be mounting a major attack on Washington after all. But like the Union leadership, they were getting the idea. A Confederate officer named

Drew Wat ("an ex-Washingtonian, well known in this city…a young man of fine promise who, mislead by bad counsels, left with other Washingtonians here to join the traitorous gang at Richmond") wrote two letters from his camp at Silver Spring, one to his mother and another to a friend, both of whom were in Washington:[185]

> *HEADQUARTERS CO. F, 23rd REGT. CAVALRY,*
> *Silver Springs* [sic], *4 miles from Washington, July 12.*
> *My Darling Mother: It seems hard that here I am within sight of my home and cannot get there. I can hardly realize that I am here; it seems like a pleasant dream to be in such a familiar place. I certainly expected to have been in Washington last night, but fate decreed otherwise, and for fear that I will not get there, I will write. I am well—have not been hurt and have been fighting almost every day. My horse has been shot from under me, but I have not been touched.*
>
> *I wonder how you all look. I would give worlds to see you all again, and I know you all want to see me, but I suppose we will have to wait till a kind Providence grants our prayer. I fixed up nicely to come to W[ashington], and if we do not get there, it will be a sore disappointment to me; but however, as a good soldier, I will have to trust in the sagacity of our dear General and valor of our boys. We have been skirmishing here all the morning, but no general engagement has taken place; when it does come off I will fight hard to come home.*
>
> *All the W[ashington] boys are well. Tell Bettie and the girls to write to me whenever they can. Give the enclosed to Billy Bayly. Love to all. Affectionately,*
> *WAT DREW, Capt. Co. F, 22d* [sic; actually the Twenty-third]
> *Reg't, Va. Cav.*

The second letter for his friend Billy Bayly, enclosed with the first, read:

> *Silver Spring, near toll gate* [on Georgia Avenue just south of Colesville Road], *July 12, 1864*
> *My Dear Will: I expected to have seen you last night, but as you see, we are doomed to disappointment. For fear that I should not succeed in seeing you, I will write. We crossed the* [Potomac] *river about a week ago, and was received by the people in this section of the state much better than I anticipated, and I assure you that I had a most glorious time. You cannot imagine how I would love to see you, and have a real good old talk. I only pray that we may meet soon.*

I have been very lucky, been fighting almost every day now for seven or eight weeks, and have never received a scratch. My horse was shot from under me at Salem, whilst [Major] Harry Gilmore and myself were charging some Yankee cavalry. I have had a fine company, and my rauster [sic] rolls show a fine record; out of 75 men who were on my rolls, I have now but 25 for duty—the rest are either killed, wounded or prisoners. At the battle of New Market my company suffered more than any in the fight, having lost two killed and seven badly wounded.

Tom Darden, Ed Jones, and Jack Everett are with me here, and all ask to be remembered. Remember me to Charley, your mother, George, your wife, and all friends. Say to the folks at home that I am all right, and hope that my usual good fortune will attend me. Faherty sends love to you and all.

Very affectionately, your friend,
WAT DREW, Capt. Co. F,
23d reg't Va. cavalry, Imboden's brigade.
W.H.C. BALY.[186]

That morning, Register of the Treasury Chittenden had applied to Secretary of War Stanton for a pass to go to Fort Stevens. He got the pass along with "an earnest warning not to use it, as a heavy battle now seems imminent on the north side of the city." Nonetheless, Chittenden ordered his Treasury clerks "to make everything snug" and then gave them the rest of the day off. He ordered his horses and light wagon to be at the Treasury at 1:00 p.m. so he could head to the fort, taking both the solicitor of the Treasury and a representative of the Jay Cooke & Company bank with him to see the excitement.[187]

So many Washingtonians wanted to see the fighting that an order had to be issued keeping them away from the forts. General Orders, No. 22, said in part: "It is hereby ordered that no person not in the Military service shall be allowed to approach the lines of defences [sic] surrounding the cities of Washington and Georgetown or to enter the camps therein without a permit signed by or by the order of the Major General Commanding the Department, or the Secretary of War. Any person so offending will be arrested and his horses, vehicles, or other property seized and condemned to Military Use."[188]

Apparently, many of the visitors to the front were fortifying themselves with alcohol before or during the trip. General Orders, No. 116, issued along with No. 22 stated, "From and after this date no spirituous or malt liquors will be allowed to be sold in the city of Washington at any place on 7th or 14th streets north of F Street. All licenses heretofore granted for the sale of liquor at any places located in the above-described territory are revoked, and any person offering liquors for sale within the prescribed limits will have the same at once confiscated, and the owners will be liable to imprisonment. Any evasion or violation of this order will be promptly and severely punished."[189] Since the city of Washington extended only as far north as today's Florida Avenue, apparently alcohol could be legally sold farther north in Washington County, but that rural area presumably had no alcohol vendors.

Despite the threats of seizure of the horses and vehicles of violators, the effort to keep sightseers away from the forts was far from successful. The *Constitutional Union* reporter who went to Fort Stevens reported that when he reached "a line of sentry placed across the road to stop civilians" within a mile of the fort, he "got by without much trouble." Many others apparently didn't have much trouble either. The reporter found "a large number of spectators assembled on the top of the hill, beside the fort, where a breastwork of rails ran across the road. The Confederates occasionally would elevate their rifles and send a ball among them. Several stampedes were thus occasioned. One of these balls struck a negro in the jaw, some sixty yards to the rear of the fort."[190]

The reporter went on to say, "On our return to town, hundreds of small boys and females were wending their way out to the front; also ice cream and cake venders [*sic*]. All seemed as though they were going to a pic nic [*sic*], instead of a scene of blood and carnage."[191]

The army finally got some control over the spectators heading toward Fort Stevens late in the afternoon. The *Evening Star* reported that about 4:00 p.m., there was a traffic jam of pedestrians, horses and vehicles, all stopped at a guard post "near the first tollgate [probably near Webster Street] to prevent civilians from going nearer to the scene of conflict."[192]

That afternoon, after a cabinet meeting, President Lincoln, who must not have seen enough the day before; Mrs. Lincoln; and Secretary of War Stanton visited a field hospital and assessed the situation at Fort Stevens firsthand. The fort was under occasional fire from Confederate sharpshooters, who had clear shots at the fort. One sharpshooter, who was firing from a location now marked by a plaque about one hundred yards west of the entrance to the later Walter Reed Army Medical Center grounds at Georgia Avenue at Butternut Street, narrowly missed hitting President Lincoln. An army surgeon, Dr. Cornelius C.V.A. Crawford, standing next to the president was

A sharpshooter's tree at the former Walter Reed Army Medical Center grounds, circa 1914. *Library of Congress.*

The sharpshooter's tree memorial at the former Walter Reed Army Medical Center grounds, now inaccessible to the public. *Allen C. Browne photo.*

hit. Mrs. Lincoln fainted. President Lincoln finally got out of the line of fire and is reported to have said that his wife would never make a good soldier if she fainted at the sight of blood. He stayed at the fort into the evening. Dr. Crawford, who survived, was reportedly the only casualty within Fort Stevens during the entire campaign.[193]

Lieutenant Colonel Hyde of the Sixth Corps described the scene:

> *I was sitting on the ramparts of Fort Stevens watching our people get into position, and looking at the flight of shells from a few great guns firing, when I saw the President standing on the wall a little way off. Bullets were whizzing over in a desultory manner, and the puffs of smoke in the woods opposite were growing in number. An officer standing on the wall between me and Mr. Lincoln suddenly keeled over and was helped away. Then a lot of people persuaded Mr. Lincoln to get down out of range, which he very reluctantly did.*[194]

Major General Horatio G. Wright of the Sixth Corps, who had invited Lincoln to join him on the parapet in the first place and who later said he didn't expect Lincoln to do it,[195] claimed he ordered Lincoln to get down:

> *I said: "Mr. President, I know you are Commander of the armies of the United States, but I am in command here, and as you are not safe where you are standing, and I am responsible for your personal safety, I order you to come down." Mr. Lincoln looked at me, smiled, and then, more in consideration of my earnestness than my instructions, stepped down and took position behind the parapet. Even then he would insist of standing up and exposing his tall form.*[196]

In 1903, William V. Cox walked the battlefield with Major General Alexander McD. McCook, who had been in overall charge of the defenses of Washington, a short time before McCook died. McCook told him that he had escorted Lincoln to the northeast section of the fort and gotten him an ammunition box to sit on so he could watch the troops charge the Confederate line. Lincoln wasn't content with sitting, regardless of the danger from sharpshooters. "When the men charged across the field toward the Reeves and Carberry [about a block west of Georgia Avenue at Butternut Street] houses through the dense copse [a group of trees] the President could not restrain himself, and was on top of the earthworks waving his hat."[197]

New York Times, January 13, 1907.

According to a first-person account in the *New York Times* in 1907, Lincoln may even have been hit by a Confederate sharpshooter as he watched the action. Colonel William P. Roome had been at Fort Stevens when Lincoln and cabinet members approached his position. He recalled:

> *They halted but a few yards from my position, at the side of the road that led from the fort…The fire from the enemy was thick and fast, and the crackling almost continuous. Most of it fell short of the enclosure, but occasionally we could hear the buzz of a bullet as it came straying over the wall and fell among us.*
>
> *While so standing, one of these bullets, fired at long range by a Confederate, struck the President on the thigh. The force was not sufficient to wound him; in fact I doubt it pierced his trousere* [sic]. *The bullet fell to the ground. President Lincoln paid no attention to it other than to glance down and permit a smile to linger for a moment on his face.*[198]

Regardless of whether Lincoln actually had been hit by a spent bullet, the fighting continued with greater or lesser intensity throughout the day and into the evening except during a heavy rainstorm that came through the area around 2:00 p.m.

The *Evening Star* commented that "for several hours…a rebel officer mounted on a horse could be seen riding in and out of the woods fronting Fort Stevens. During all this time he was a perfect target for our men, but attempts to dismount him proved fruitless." Other Confederates were not so lucky. "A member of the 76th New York regiment took up a position in a tree from which he picked off six of the rebel sharpshooters."[199]

Union forces defending the forts finally tired of the Rebels using houses north of the forts for cover. The widow Carberry's house and the Claggett house (in the area near Fourteenth and Jonquil Streets, NW) were destroyed by Union shelling, as reported in the *Constitutional Union*:

> *Between 6 and 7 o'clock…the Confederate sharpshooters who had possession of the widow Carberry's dwelling out on the Seventh Street Pike beyond Fort Stevens, became very annoying, and it was determined by General McCook to dislodge them. The line of battle was formed by a portion of the Sixth Corps, and advanced a short distance up the road. A shell was sent out from the fort which exploded in the house; throwing bricks and wood work around in great confusion. The Confederate sharpshooters decamped at once…The federal troops pushed on until they reached a house on the right of the road* [probably the Daly house or the Cuttings house], *where a large number of Confederates ensconced themselves and began to fire out the windows. This house was soon captured with all its inmates. Very little of the Confederates was seen after this as they left in a great hurry. At the house of F.P. Blair, sr., at Silver Springs* [sic] *they left one hundred and one of their wounded, including eleven officers…The widow Carberry's and the Claggett residence have both been destroyed, and it is further reported that the Blair mansion was burned this morning; but we do not believe this, as the Confederates left their wounded in it.*[200]

The *Evening Star* provided additional details, noting that "the skillful gunners of the 6th Maine artillery" sent a shell from Fort Stevens that "lodged in the cupola of the Carberry house, firing the building and sending the rebels skedaddling from its shelter like so many rats."[201]

The Union infantry charge in coordination with an artillery barrage from both Fort Stevens and Fort DeRussy came at dusk. Union troops led a bayonet charge against the Confederate skirmish line north of the fort on both sides of Georgia Avenue. Most of Early's troops were massed farther back and to the sides. As the Union troops pressed forward beyond the skirmish line, Confederate resistance stiffened, and Confederate artillery opened up on the advancing Union forces. A firefight broke out around the later site of the Walter Reed Army Medical Center. Union reinforcements and more ammunition had to be brought up. At one point, a Union unit being pushed back by the Confederates charged despite being out of ammunition. They drove the Confederates back and held their position until more ammunition arrived.

As the skirmish finally wound down around 10:00 p.m., well after dark, Union forces had driven the Confederates back about a mile toward Francis Preston Blair's "Silver Spring" mansion and had held the battlefield. The *National Intelligencer* said (probably erroneously) that the advance went even farther, claiming, "The rebels were driven a mile or more, and completely dislodged from their skirmishing position, and our line advanced beyond the house of Mr. F.P. Blair."[202]

Regardless of how far they advanced, the Union troops had suffered unusually high losses. From 250 to 375 Union troops had been killed or wounded out of about 1,000 in the unit that had led the assault. The casualty rate was said to be about twice the average for the Battles of Antietam, Chancellorsville and Gettysburg. The Confederates claimed lower losses; Early admitted to only 80 casualties for both July 11 and 12, although another source says the "best estimate" of Confederates killed, wounded or captured totaled 500 men.[203]

Register of the Treasury Chittenden, who had stayed near Fort Stevens all afternoon and went out into the area retaken by Union forces, described the scene after the battle in his *Recollections*:

> *The fighting was over, but the experiences of the day were not yet ended. I went back to my horses, found them well cared for, and then went on to the field of battle. Men with stretchers were already carrying off the wounded and collecting the dead. A few yards beyond our works I met two men. One, tall and powerful, was leaning heavily upon the other, a boy who was carrying the guns of both. The former asked me if I knew where the field hospital was? After directing him to it I inquired where he was hurt. He replied by opening his shirt and exposing the path of a minie-bullet directly through his chest. I took his name and afterwards traced him, found that he recovered, and was, when last heard from, a healthy man. His surgeon said that the wound was received during the exhalation of air from his lungs. Had the ball entered the lungs during inhalation, the wound must have been fatal.*[204]

He also said the houses that had been hit by Union shells burned very slowly and that "on all the floors, on the roofs, in the yards, within reach of the heat, were many bodies of the dead or dying, who could not move, and had been left behind by their comrades. The odor of burning flesh filled the air; it was a sickening spectacle!"[205]

Chittenden described a dead Confederate officer:

Near a large fallen tree lay one in the uniform of an officer. His sword was by his side, but his hand grasped a rifle. What could have sent an officer here to act as a sharp-shooter? I placed my hand on his chest to detect any sign of life. It encountered a metallic substance. I opened his clothing, and took from beneath it a shield of boiler-iron, moulded [sic] *to fit the anterior portion of his body, and fastened at the back by straps and buckles. Trusting to this protection, he had gone out that morning gunning for Yankees. In the language of a quaint epitaph in Vernon, Vt., upon one who died from vaccination,*

> *"The means employed his life to save,*
> *Hurried him headlong to the grave!"*

Directly over his heart, through the shield and through his body, was a hole large enough to permit the escape of a score of human lives.[206]

He continued with the description of a dead Confederate sharpshooter:

There behind the log, he lay, on his back, his eyes open gazing upwards, with a peaceful expression on his rugged face. In the middle of his forehead was the small wound which had ended his career. A single crimson line led from it, along his face, to where the blood dropped upon the ground. A minie-rifle, discharged, was grasped in his right hand; a box, with a single remaining cartridge, was fast to his side. The rifle and cartridge-box were of English make, and the only things about him which did not indicate extreme destitution. His feet, wrapped in rags, had coarse shoes upon them, so worn and full of holes that they were only held together by many pieces of thick twine. Ragged trousers, a jacket, and a shirt of what used to be called "tow-cloth" [a coarse, heavy linen], *a straw hat, which had lost a large portion of both crown and rim, completed his attire. His hair was a mat of dust and dirt, which gave him the color of the red Virginia clay.*

A haversack hung from his shoulder. Its contents were a jack-knife, a plug of twisted tobacco, a tin cup, and about two quarts of coarsely cracked corn, with, perhaps, an ounce of salt, tied in a rag. My notes made the next day, say that this corn had been ground upon the cob, making the provender which the Western farmer feeds to his cattle. This was a complete inventory of the belongings of one Confederate soldier.[207]

Although the skirmishing had ended, the Union forces didn't get much rest. Union gunners continued occasional artillery fire, and the troops "rested on their arms during the night in the forts and rifle-pits." They were up and in line by 3:00 a.m.[208]

Meanwhile, that night, Early began his withdrawal toward the Potomac River and the perceived safety of the Virginia countryside. As they retreated, someone set fire to Postmaster General Montgomery Blair's twelve-year-old "Falkland" mansion. Early would later deny it was done by his troops, at least not by his order. J.E. Turton, the contractor working at "Falkland" who had been captured by the Confederates the day before, said, "The rebels began to leave the vicinity of Silver Spring about 9 o'clock Tuesday night and at 11 o'clock they set fire to the house of Montgomery Blair, as their rear was moving away." Turton also said that they didn't threaten him but "took his change of clothing, and on his remonstrating, they said 'We can't help it; you are where you can get plenty; we can't.'"[209] "However, they did not attempt to steal the fifty dollars he had with him."[210]

One of the last retreating Confederate soldiers later all but confirmed that they had burned "Falkland" but justified the act. He said, "As we marched by the Blair house it was wrapped in flames. No one knows who fired it.

Tourists examine the ruins of "Falkland" after the Confederate retreat. Montgomery Blair rebuilt the home. It was burned again on September 7, 1958, this time by the Silver Spring Volunteer Fire Department, which was asked to burn it to clear the site for construction of the Blair Plaza shopping center and apartments. *Library of Congress.*

Some say it was set on fire by the enemy's shells, but this could not be, for their aim was too high. Others say it was done by General Early's orders, but he denied after the war that he had it done. I suspect it was done by some of our men who were exasperated by the numerous wanton crimes of the Federal soldiers in the South."[211]

In 1881, Early doubted that his troops were responsible for the burning of "Falkland": "I had placed a guard over that house also [in addition to Francis Preston Blair's "Silver Spring"], and it was not burned by my orders, but was fired after my guard had been withdrawn. I have never been able to ascertain who did the burning."[212] He went on to say:

> *General Rodes, whose division occupied my front line, and furnished the guard for the house, was of [the] opinion that it was burned by some resident of the neighborhood, who took advantage of our presence to commit the act. It is not impossible that the burning was by some of my men, but it was without my authority. It was my policy to prohibit everything like marauding on the part of my troops, and I was especially determined to prevent the destruction of the property of the Blairs, for it was understood that both the father and the son were opposed to the policy pursued by some Federal commanders in the South in the destruction of private property and the imprisonment of non-combatant citizens. In fact, it was understood by us that Montgomery Blair had lost caste with the extreme Radicals of the party to which he was attached at that time, and it was not a great while before he retired from the Cabinet. There is a citizen of one of the upper counties of the Valley, who is still living [in 1881], who had followed my command into Maryland, and who came to me while I was in front of Washington with the request that I would permit him to burn the house of Montgomery Blair, in retaliation for the burning of many houses in the Valley by General Hunter's orders. This permission I refused, with a statement of my reasons therefor.*[213]

It might have been easy for someone to burn "Falkland" regardless of any orders. The retreat was apparently not well organized. A Union POW said that just after he and his fellow prisoners had been taken to the rear under heavy guard, "the whole rebel army came pell mell, almost a stampede," with infantry and drovers herding captured livestock fleeing north through the fields and the cavalry and artillery units heading back up Georgia Avenue.[214]

Early later justified his retreat, saying that staying any longer would have resulted in the loss of his entire army:

My small force had been thrown up to the very walls of the Federal Capital, north of a river which could not be forded at any point within 40 miles, and with a heavy force and the South Mountain in my rear—the passes through which mountain could be held by a small number of troops. A glance at the map, when it is recollected that the Potomac is a wide river, and navigable to Washington for the largest vessels, will cause the intelligent reader to wonder, not why I failed to take Washington but why I had the audacity to approach it as I did, with the small force under my command.[215]

After deciding to withdraw, Early is reported to have said, "We haven't taken Washington, but we've scared Abe Lincoln like hell!"[216]

The last detachment of two hundred Confederates left after midnight. They had been ordered to hold the line while the rest of the troops withdrew. Then they were to serve as a rear guard until the cavalry fell in behind them.[217]

Chapter 10

EARLY'S RETREAT

B y Wednesday morning, July 13, the Confederate army was on its way back to the Shenandoah Valley.

Captured Union artificer Nelson A. Fitts recalled, "On the 12th, about sundown, we [the Confederates] left Seventh street in a hurry, marched to Rockville, getting there at daylight on the 13th; halted half an hour, and then went on until 2 p.m. then stopped until dark. We followed the line of the telegraph from Rockville to Poolesville, halted on the Maryland side until light."[218]

Not all the Union prisoners "marched" to Rockville. One of them later recalled "one noble act of the rebs, who have so much cruelty charged to their account. My friend Burton had been very sick that day [July 12] and was too weak to walk, and I obtained permission from a rebel surgeon to allow him to ride in an ambulance, while many of their men wounded and worn had to walk in that July heat and dust."[219]

The Union forces were ignorant of the Confederate retreat until early Wednesday morning. The first report of the retreat came from Fort Stevens at 6:10 a.m.: "The enemy have disappeared from the entire front. All the disposable cavalry have started on this and the Rockville road to learn which route he has taken."[220]

Union major general McCook later filed a summary report saying that he sent out two companies of infantry to find out what had happened. He then went forward himself and saw "nothing but the deserted camps of the enemy, and a few stragglers; also a hospital at Sligo Post-Office containing about 70

Early's forces retreating across the Potomac with captured supplies and livestock. "Early Recrossing the Potomac." Alfred H. Guernsey and Henry M. Alden, *Harper's Pictorial History of the Civil War* 2 (Chicago: Puritan Press Co., 1894), 708.

rebels wounded too severely to be moved, 11 of them commissioned officers, including surgeons and attendants—about 90 in all."[221] McCook's troops took at least 200 Confederate prisoners between Fort Stevens and Wheaton, including those at the hospital. He estimated the Confederates had lost at least 250 killed and wounded, which was about the Union losses and on the low end of other estimates.[222]

There were also other somewhat conflicting reports. Major General Christopher Columbus Augur reported from Fort Stevens at 8:30 a.m. on Wednesday, July 13, that the Confederates had left "a hospital there [Sligo] of ninety men and eleven officers in charge of two medical officers. Mr. Montgomery Blair's place ["Falkland"] is burned. The old gentleman's

THE POTOMAC.

[Francis Preston Blair's "Silver Spring"] is not burned...A good many of their dead are unburied."[223] The *Evening Star* also reported that the rebels "left their dead of that fight upon the field."[224]

There initially was confusion as to where the Confederate hospital had been located. For example, a report to General Grant at 1:15 p.m. said it had been at Francis Preston Blair's "Silver Spring." The report also noted that other "wounded [were] also left on the ground in front of Fort Stevens."[225] Another report said that about two hundred additional Confederate wounded were found between Sligo and Leesborough (Wheaton).[226]

Major General Barnard's later summary report noted that William Batchelor had watched the retreat all night from the front porch of his house on the east side of Georgia Avenue north of Forest Glen Road. The Confederate rear guard, which had camped near his home, started retreating with its wagons at about 7:00 p.m. Troops passed his home heading north continuously, except for "three halts of about fifteen minutes each," until 5:00 a.m., when the last troops, about two thousand cavalry, went by.[227]

Major General McCook reported from Fort Stevens at noon on July 13: "Captain Taylor, of cavalry detachment, reports from Leesborough [Wheaton] that the enemy moved to the left to Rockville; 200 wagons and 2,000 head of cattle. A general told the citizens they were going to Muddy Branch and Leesburg."[228]

That afternoon, the *Evening Star* confirmed the retreat into Virginia: "Information reached here at half-past 1 today, by Scouts from up river, that the rebels were this morning recrossing the Potomac nearly opposite Poolsville. They were driving before them 2,000 head of cattle, which they had stolen." The *Evening Star* also reported, "In addition to their work of plunder and devastation, we hear that they have been forcing nearly every able-bodied man they have been able to pick up in Maryland into their ranks, carrying them off with them." A later report said the booty included "several thousand head of cattle and a large number of horses."[229]

Some Union troops were sent out after the Confederates and caught up with their rear guard in Rockville. During a running engagement through Rockville, over ninety Rebels were taken prisoner, but the Union pursuers did not follow up. Early's troops easily escaped to Virginia with his captured livestock, supplies and prisoners to fight another day.

A few Rebel stragglers were captured after Early's troops headed back across the Potomac. The *Evening Star* reported on several who were captured by one lucky, or perhaps unlucky, Union cavalryman who had somehow lost his regiment:

Andrew Myers of company M, 13th Penn. cavalry, having got separated from his regiment, left the city on Wednesday to rejoin the same. When several miles from the city he came upon two rebel soldiers, who he took prisoners by presenting a revolver to their heads and demanding their surrender. He brought his prisoners to this city and turned them over to Provost Marshal Ingraham, and on Thursday morning again started on his journey, but had not proceeded far before he overtook two more "Johnnies," who he took prisoners also, and again returned to Col. Ingraham's office, where he delivered up his charge. Yesterday morning Myers made another attempt to overtake his command, but strange to say, when between Tennallytown and Rockville he fell in with four more of the rebel stragglers, whom he ordered to "about face" and march to Washington. Myers accompanied his prisoners to the city, where they were committed to the Old Capitol [prison] *to keep the company of those previously captured by the dashing cavalryman.*[230]

Even though a few Rebels were mopped up as their army retreated, the fact that the bulk of Early's army was allowed to escape so easily continued to be a matter of consternation for both President Lincoln and his wife. When Secretary of War Stanton told Mary Todd Lincoln that he was going to have a full-length portrait painted of her standing on the ramparts to see the battle at Fort Stevens, she is reputed to have told him, "I can assure you of one thing, Mr. Secretary, if I had had a few *ladies* with me the Rebels would not have been permitted to get away as they did!"[231] The portrait wasn't painted.

Some Confederate dead were gathered and buried on the Osborn farm near the fort.[232] Many others, no doubt, remain lost where they were initially buried near where they fell. Forty Union dead were buried at the new Battleground National Cemetery on the east side of Georgia Avenue between Whittier Place and Van Buren Street, about a half mile north of Fort Stevens.

The troops Grant sent to reinforce Washington were sent back to Virginia to once again aid in the efforts against Richmond.

The civilian quartermaster employees were relieved from the trenches on Thursday, July 14, and ordered to march back to Washington and resume their regular duties. But they weren't fully demobilized. An order was issued that "the organization of the clerks, workmen, and laborers of the Quartermaster's Department will be kept up; and to make it more efficient a certain time should be devoted to drill at regular periods." All quartermaster employees were to wear a Quartermaster Department badge; badges of "those who actually took the field during the late demonstrations against Washington" were to have a special red cloth border.[233]

In his order sending his quartermaster employees back to their normal duties, quartermaster general Meigs said that he took this opportunity "to thank the soldiers and the civilians of the Quartermaster's Department for the alacrity and zeal with which they organized and moved to defend the capital, insulted by traitors. The rebel army, under tried and skillful leaders, has looked at and has felt of the northern defenses of Washington. These looked ugly and felt hard. They left their dead unburied, and many of their wounded on the way by which they retired. They will not soon again insult the majesty of a free people in their nation's capital."[234]

Two of the quartermaster civilian employees became casualties during the fighting. One suffered a slight arm wound, but another, who was actually a former employee accompanying his former colleagues as a volunteer, "was shot through the body and almost instantly killed." In total, about 2,700 civilian quartermaster employees had been mobilized. In addition to their efforts north of Washington, some protected government facilities and stores in the Alexandria area.[235]

Quartermaster general Meigs noted in a report that despite mobilizing 2,700 of his civilian employees, the Quartermaster Department had fitted out "the troops arriving from Petersburg and New Orleans with horses, wagons and artillery. We mounted 2,000 or 3,000 cavalry; gave 1,000 or 2,000 horses to horse artillery batteries; supplied 15,000 men with a new wagon train, and mounted most of the general officers and started them, a well-equipped movable column in pursuit [of Early after the battle]."[236]

A few troops remained to defend Washington after most had been sent back south. For the remaining troops, it was not altogether pleasant duty despite the fact that fresh food could be gotten from local farms. Troops camped at Fort Reno claimed the bedbugs there were "the largest, fiercest and most numerous yet encountered."[237]

There was other good news in addition to the Rebel retreat. The city's only rail connection with the rest of the country would soon be restored. The damage was much less than previously believed. The *Evening Star* reported that an engine dispatched north to reconnoiter the track at Bladensburg "found a railroad man who had come from the Relay House [a hotel located where the Washington branch of the B&O Railroad joined the main line just north of the Patapsco River, east of the intersection of today's I-95 and I-895] this morning and learned from him that the rebels had failed to damage the road to any serious extent. They had set fire to the tressel-work [*sic*] at Paint Branch [at the northwest corner of today's College Park Airport] but it did not burn, the timbers being only slightly scorched. None of the other bridges, or any portion of the track, had been injured to any appreciable extent. We may expect the speedy resumption of travel on the road."[238]

The railroad was also on the mind of Secretary of War Stanton. At 9:30 p.m., he sent a dispatch to John W. Garrett, president of the B&O Railroad, telling him, "There is no reason your trains should not commence immediately their usual trips. This morning I ordered Colonel McCallum to put his whole available force on your road to repair damage." He explained, "The enemy having learned yesterday the arrival of troops from City Point and New Orleans, retreated in the night towards Edwards Ferry. The appearance of their camp indicates a hasty departure. Their dead were left unburied, and their sick in the camp hospitals…There is no reason to doubt that the whole force has been withdrawn from this region, and is retreating across the Potomac."[239]

News of Early's attack and the burning of the "Falkland" mansion—or, more likely, earlier rumors of the burning of the "Silver Spring" mansion—apparently had spread before news of Early's retreat. Elizabeth Blair Lee wrote her husband from Cape May, New Jersey, on July 13:

> *My dear Phil,*
> *Mother is very much overcome by the burning of Silver Spring* [she apparently had heard erroneous rumors that her father's "Silver Spring" mansion had been burned] *and the terror felt about the safety of my father, whom we learn had returned to Washington. It is very hard, but as long as God spares our dear ones and covers their precious heads in battle, I cannot grieve even for a home where everything is as dear to me as at Silver Spring. Each bush and tree has had my care and watching in that lawn. Still if our Capitol is not dishonored and my husband and brother are brought safe through all these hardships and battles, I shall be thankful and I will try to let no other feeling come into my heart.*[240]

News of Early's retreat still had not yet reached Elizabeth Blair Lee a day later. She wrote her husband on Thursday, July 14:

> *If the Rebels had massed on Washington as we left it, they had little to do but walk in. The total blindness and stupidity about this invasion was extraordinary. Any hint on my part of such a possibility was met with a scorn that withered my courage for any action but to get away with my sick mother.*
> *I got nearly every article of clothing and all that was my own except my writing desk and work box, which have nothing in them. As I came downstairs with them in my arms, I met mother and again urged that the silver at least might be taken to the City. No, she would not have the house pulled to pieces. Then I said well I'll send some plated ware in its place, to which she assented. I put down my boxes and went to work after the silver. Then I was hurried off as we were late as usual. In my haste left my dear old boxes. Your letters I had taken the day before; the bulk of them are always kept there by me. I shrink from being an alarmist but under the derision and even secession cast upon me, I had not the whim to rise. I think father, Mr. Fox, and brother will recollect with some pain my entreaties to them not to go away. The truth is the fatuity* [smug stupidity] *is not yet*

over, for the Times *of yesterday is out with the meanest article precisely in the same contemptuous tone as to the enemy and their force in Maryland and that in the same columns announcing the capitol is cut off from the rest of the country. Such people are good allies of our foe.*[241]

By this time, of course, the residents of Washington knew what was going on. The news of the retreat was a major change from the rumors circulating Wednesday morning that Confederate general Longstreet had thirty thousand more troops at Falls Church ready to join the attack from the west. The Confederates also had been rumored to be building an artillery battery at Matthias Point on the Potomac River north of Dahlgren, Virginia. The battery wouldn't have immediately threatened Washington, but it would have allowed them to impede Union reinforcements from coming up the Potomac and would have further isolated Washington, which had already lost rail and telegraph links to the rest of the country.[242]

Even before the news of the retreat was widely known, the head of the British legation, Lord Richard Bickerton Pemell Lyons, wasn't terribly concerned, at least for himself. He wrote his sister on the thirteenth that "there is a large Confederate force within three or four miles of Washington, and some say they will make an attempt to take the town today…Even if the town was taken my physical comfort would not be likely to be disturbed. I don't really expect to have to move, and I daresay you will hear next week that things have lapsed into their odious condition [his view of what was normal in Washington]."[243]

Despite Lord Lyons' confidence that things would return to normal, the Union military leadership wasn't so sure. The *National Intelligencer* reported that various volunteers and city militia had mustered on Wednesday, July 13, in accordance with previous orders, but none was accepted into service except for clerks and employees of the Interior Department. About one hundred men of the "National Rifles," which had served in 1861, were going to be mustered into service on Thursday, as were several companies from the "Union League." In addition, "Clerks and Employees of the Department of Agriculture have formed themselves into a military organization at the suggestion of the Commissioner, Hon. Isaac Newton. They have received arms, equipment, and ammunition, and have commenced drilling vigorously."[244]

There was continuing fear that Washington might face Confederate threats. Chief of Staff Halleck wrote General Grant on July 19 that Early's raid showed that circumstances had changed, and he wanted more troops stationed in the Washington area because the "garrisons of Washington and Baltimore are made up of troops entirely unfit for the field and wholly inadequate for the defense of these places…If the enemy had crossed the Potomac below Harpers Ferry (and it is now fordable in many places), and had moved directly upon Washington or Baltimore, or if the arrival of the Sixth Corps had been delayed twenty-four hours, one or the other of these places, with their large depots of supplies, would have been in very considerable danger. Will it be safe to have this risk repeated? Is not Washington too important in a political as well as a military point of view to run any serious risk at all? I repeat that so long as Lee is able to make any larger detachments, Washington cannot be deemed safe without a larger and more available force in its vicinity."[245]

On July 26 and 27, there was particular fear of another attack on Washington, and Grant shifted some troops back toward Washington. Two days later, on the twenty-ninth, "stringent orders…concerning stealing from the inhabitants and leaving camp" were issued, and an extended drill was ordered. There was another scare on August 1, two days after cavalry under Early burned Chambersburg, Pennsylvania. The War Department "sent the men into the forts to their guns for several following days."[246]

Elizabeth Blair Lee, who had returned to "Silver Spring," was among those fearful of another attack. On August 1, she wrote to her husband: "I have been busy cutting and fixing house linen and working over the details of this house and yet with a terror in my heart of another visit by the Rebs, which I do not think improbable. I would not be surprised if Lee evacuated Richmond and came en masse here to die out with effect if the rumors are true of the destruction and capture of Petersburg."[247]

A week later, she apparently was no longer fearful. She had met General Grant on her way home from church. She told her husband that Grant "recognized me more promptly than I did him, and we chatted 15 minutes." She told him that she had "slept soundly from a new sense of security" the night before.[248]

Ultimately, the fear that Lee would detach more of his forces to attack Washington was not realized. Early was routed by Major General Philip H. Sheridan's Army of the Shenandoah at the Battle of Cedar Creek on October 19, ending the Confederates' ability to operate effectively in the Shenandoah Valley or attack the North through the valley. Washington was never again seriously threatened.

Chapter 11

THE BATTLE'S AFTERMATH

D espite some continuing fears, Lord Lyons had been essentially correct. Things soon returned to what had been normal before Early's raid, except that now residents had a new recreational option. Touring the battlefield became a popular activity. The *Evening Star* provided an account:

THE REBEL INVERSION [sic]

To go out the 7ᵗʰ street road was the correct thing yesterday [Wednesday, July 13]. *Supposing you couldn't afford a horse—with flour at $25 a barrel—there were the street cars to the Boundary* [today's Florida Avenue], *thence on foot. We went out. It is proper, we see by our morning contemporaries* [presumably a reference to the *Constitutional Union*], *to note progress by the yard in going out the 7ᵗʰ street road. Thus we. At the Boundary our progress was barred by difficulty in getting lager. There was no getting to the front without lager, and no lager to be had. There were bars in plenty, (7ᵗʰ street north is lined with them,) and lager in plenty, but "not a drop to drink,"—military orders against it. The bar-keepers looked sorry and we looked sorry.*

There were some soldiers coming from the rear entrance of a restaurant wiping their mouths. We went in and came out wiping our mouth. Bar-keeper there evidently hadn't heard of the order. Then we walked up a hill. Something smelt bad. We thought it was dead rebels. It proved to be Bell's slaughter-house. At the right, on the brow of the hill, were some burnt

The Old Tavern by Nicolai Cikovsky shows the artist's conception of Union troops at Sligo, the intersection of Georgia Avenue and Colesville Road, after the Confederates retreated. The mural was commissioned for the Silver Spring Post Office in 1937 and was later moved to the Silver Spring Library. *Photo by the author.*

timbers in ruins—invasion ruins doubtless. We got out our note book. A New York "Special" was ahead of us. He had dismounted from his horse, he was down upon his knees and was examining the relics through his eye-glass. Some objects there looked like the bones of a human being. This human being had perished in the flames. Thus was the horrors of war. We asked an 8th Illinois cavalry man about it. He thought the bones were beef bones. The ruins were those of a shed burned by accident a year or more ago. The Special put up his eye-glass. We put up our note book, firmly resolved to draw it no more until there was something to note.

FORT STEVENS AND OUTSIDE.

Passing Fort Stevens there were indications of war in earnest. Gaunt chimney stacks standing amid smoking ruins to the right of a peach orchard just

felled (after the enemy were gone,) to the left, some distance away, the blaze
of a conflagration, where the fire from a building fired by the Confederates
in leaving had spread through the underbrush enveloping a dwelling house.
The fire was yet smouldering in the Lay house ruins [the Thomas Lay
house, which had been "a fine wooden mansion, two stories
in height, with a cupola,"[249] was east of Georgia Avenue at
approximately today's Dahlia Street; his farm extended west
into what became the Walter Reed Army Medical Center site],
as shown by a thin spiral of smoke rising over a clump of shrubbery. It is
difficult to realize that not 24 hours ago the rebels were hiding in this house
with such impudent temerity directly under the guns of our fortifications.

In fact they were yet nearer the fort, occupying positions behind knolls,
bushes, and trees, within three hundred yards of Fort Stevens. Here it was
the veterans of the 6th corps, spreading themselves out in fan-form line of
skirmishers, advanced with the audacity gained from previous baptism in
fire, across the open field, directly under the deadly fire from those leafy
coverts. On they advanced, sweeping past the Lay house on the right, and
throwing up rifle-pits at once, which they hid through the night, and on the

left pushing up to the white fence of the Lay house, or rather its blazing ruins, when the rebels sent two reinforcing brigades, pushing our skirmishers back on that side.

It is a bit of display on their part of a bold front as at that very hour, 7 o'clock Tuesday night, the main portion of their force were stealing away towards the fords of the Potomac. They left in the fields some 90 of their dead, and a detail of contrabands sent out to bury them, came marching in at sunset bearing trophies of rebel guns, etc. One rebel was found buried so hastily by his comrades in their exit, that the feet were sticking out of the ground.

In the hospital tents beyond the third tollgate, the rebels left sixty-three of their wounded including eleven officers, none of them being advanced beyond the rank of captain. With these wounded they left a surgeon and two assistants surgeons, twelve nurses (soldiers) and a chaplain. Three wounded were looked after yesterday by Dr. Waters, of this city, Hospital Inspector, and they are to be removed to Lincoln Hospital [the city's largest military hospital, located at Fifteenth and East Capital Streets]. [A report from Major General McCook late on Wednesday, July 13, said he had "cleared out the rebel hospital except about thirty men impossible to move. Sent to Lincoln Hospital."][250]

The rebel General Holmes was seriously wounded at the battle of Monocacy on Saturday, and was brought with them by the rebels. He was not doing well when the rebels left, and it was not practicable to remove him. It is believed that he has been left concealed at the home of some rebel sympathizer. Strict search will be made for him. [This was an error; Confederate general Theophilus H. Holmes was not involved in Early's campaign.]

The house of Francis P. Blair ["Silver Spring"] *was occupied as headquarters by Gen. Breckinridge and was not injured.*

It has been stated by a morning contemporary [presumably a reference to the *Constitutional Union*] *that the private papers of Mr. Blair were spared by the rebels. This is a mistake. Mr. Blair's home was thoroughly ransacked, all drawers, bureaus, writing cases, etc., being forced open and their contents not carried off were thrown about the house. Mr. Blair's papers, and even the letters of the ladies of the family, were thus treated. It is not known what portion of Mr. Blair's papers were carried off, but as they were evidently all handled, it is presumed that such as bore on public affairs were stolen, as was all the plate, silver ware, etc., in the house.*

>	*A valuable picture at the Blair house was cut from the frame and carried away by some rebel vandal. The house of Montgomery Blair, with all its valuable furniture, was burned by the rebels.*
>
>	*The Rev. Mr. Macneheimer occupied the Morrison house, and was obliged to leave his sick bed in fleeing from the rebels. He loses all his furniture, clerical robes, plate, library of 800 volumes, etc., etc.*
>
>	*The story that Mr. F.P. Blair was at his residence while the rebels were there is untrue.*
>
>	*Reports brought down the road by farmers all go to show that the rebel sympathizers in Maryland were the principal sufferers by the rebel raid. Not only were their horses and cattle taken by the rebels for "the good of the cause," but they were impressed themselves into the Confederate service.*[251]

The reporter from the *Evening Star* was only one of many tourists to go to Fort Stevens on July 13. Among the others were Robert Todd Lincoln and John Hay, President Lincoln's assistant private secretary who was Robert Todd Lincoln's frequent companion in Washington. Colonel Oliver Wendell Holmes took them to where some of the Confederates had been camped. They had lunch at Montgomery Meigs' field headquarters. Later, they watched a group of fifty freedmen walk the battlefield and bring in the dead for burial.[252]

In addition to the tourists, Union troops also swept through the Sligo area on Wednesday morning, July 13. For the next few days, they searched house to house throughout the area. They found more wounded Confederates and took about three hundred prisoners. Fearing a Confederate return, they destroyed anything that might give the returning army cover. Homes north of the fort not destroyed by shelling were burned. Shade trees were cut down; several peach orchards were cleared. All this was in addition to the substantial clearing of the area in front of the fort that had been done when Fort Stevens was built. Local residents complained for years about their treatment after the battle by Union troops.[253]

Within a few days, there were many more reports of post-battle conditions in Silver Spring and near the fort.

On Friday, July 15, Francis Preston Blair arrived in Cape May, New Jersey, with definitive news for his wife and daughter Elizabeth about what had happened at "Silver Spring." He had left Washington on Wednesday on the B&O in a special car with Treasury secretary Salmon P. Chase. Elizabeth wrote to her husband the next day:

"Sack of the Blair Mansion—Rebels Carousing Near the Garden Vase.—From a Sketch by Our Special Artist, E.F. Mullen." *Frank Leslie's Illustrated Newspaper* 18, no. 462 (August 6, 1864), 305. *Library of Congress.*

Our losses by the Rebels are so small that we can never think of the invasion without a sense of escape and thankfulness. All of the crops were left just as they found them; that is at least $6000 to us. All the horses are saved but two. Mr. Harvey and the servants saved the rest. The mules, Jesup's pony, Woody's and Blair's donkey, cart and harness, and the light farm wagon are gone. The books are terribly scattered; papers ditto. All the servants ran away leaving their clothes. We found the lawn strewed with dirty rags and every article of clothing gone. Thanks to Minna Andrews too. Mother sent his clothing to the city and she packed them back instead of next door as she might have done—and where she sends both Wood and Andrew—but they have lost their house which cost them at least $14,000. The water work and out houses and grounds improvement makes a loss to them of $20,000.—

Our grapery was untouched and not a tree or shrub was injured. On the mantle in the Library, where lately received picture of General Dix was put, just below the General's figure is written: "A confederate officer, for himself and all his comrades, regrets exceedingly that damage and pilfering was committed in this house, before it was known that it was within our lines, or that private property was imperiled. Especially we regret that the Ladies property has been disturbed, but restitution has been made, and punishment meted out as far as possible. We wage no ignoble warfare for plunder or revenge, but for all that men hold dearest, and scorn to retaliate in kind the unmentioned outrage committed on our homes by federal Straps, of which the burning of [Virginia] *Governor Letcher's, Col Anderson's, and hundreds of private houses are but light matters in comparison with the darker crimes that remain untold." On a photograph of Auntie Mason (General Buell's stepdaughter) was written: "A Confederate officer has remained here until after eleven* [during the retreat on the night of July 12–13] *to prevent pillage and burning of the house because of his love of Emma Mason* [the wife of Union major general Frank Wheaton], *who found in this home good and true friends.*[254]

Mrs. Beale told father that the officers who ate at her house told her that John Breckinridge preserved Silver Spring and made more fuss about things there than if they had belonged to Jeff Davis. It had been his place of refuge and rest, etc. [Breckinridge was a Blair cousin and had often visited "Silver Spring" before the war.] *Thus bread cast upon the waters came back to us to which I can say they were welcome to return for their good offices—Blair is well but doesn't like to part with his donkey and ponies and is in a hurry to go home…*

Father left Mr. Smith in charge of the house and farm. My conclusion is that if our own Army had swarmed over us and encamped there for two days, it would have been quite as bad for us. Consequently we may well congratulate ourselves.[255]

Gideon Welles, who toured the Silver Spring area on Sunday, July 17, confirmed the general accuracy of Elizabeth Blair Lee's conclusion. Writing in his diary, he said that Blair's estate was in better condition than he had expected and that he thought the Confederates had probably gone out of their way to preserve shrubbery and crops. The house was closed, so he couldn't inspect it, but he said his son, who was in the army, had been the first to enter the house after the Confederates had left and found some papers scattered about. Welles also noted that "there had been crowds of persons there filling the house, sleeping on the floors, prying into the family privacy, but not more rudely, perhaps than our own soldiers would have done, had the place been in their power."[256]

Elizabeth's letter to her husband on July 17 noted another loss: "Blair wants to go home; bears his losses sorrowfully. A rebel shot his dog and stole his donkey cart and harness. He feels like an injured boy." Five days later, she wrote that she had seen Blair gather "up a huge quantity of pebbles, large whole ones." When she told him he couldn't take all of them home, he said, "Please let me Mama I want to put them on old Ned's grave. I know Uncle Dick has buried him, and he was a brave old dog. He fought the Rebs to the last."[257]

She provided additional details about the fate of the mansion's contents in a letter from Cape May dated July 19, saying that all usable clothes had been taken and that they would have to replace sheets, towels and everything that weighed less than a mattress. The only things not stolen or destroyed were "some blankets which escaped, I suppose, because they were in the room used by Breckinridge." They had been placed there for washing. "Mother has even her best blankets washed once a year, and these are her best ones."[258] Another letter noted that the Confederates had left the demijohns of good old bourbon empty under the table and cleaned out the larder and poultry.[259]

Elizabeth Blair Lee finally returned to "Silver Spring" on July 27, having been in Washington the previous day on her way back from Cape May. She described conditions and her son's reunion with his dog, which hadn't been killed after all:

[Blair's] *meeting with his old dog was sweet. You never saw such great joy… The dog hid and did not return here for over a week. General Breckinridge recovered Blair's donkey and put it in Jimmy Byrnes care, from whom it was stolen again. Ned Byrnes* [the deaf son of Francis Preston Blair's first nurse, Martha Byrnes Cook, who lived with the Blairs in 1864 and was being trained as a gardener][260] *went into the Fort and fought. He came out in the battle, and his display of courage is the talk of the soldiers. Mr. Smith says 15 or 16 of them spoke of his courage and skill as a sharpshooter with my Fathers rifle. After such scenes it strike me with wonder to see him whistling along joyously with Blair, in whose eyes he is now a great hero, as also he is in the eyes of some of the older men. Andrew says that the soldiers say he killed some five or six Rebel sharpshooters. I do not like to think of anybody so young taking the lives of so many men. Of course I say this to you only. But this young gardener of mine is no common boy. He has shown marked character from infancy.*

As to the house, it is in marvelously good condition. The books, the pictures, mirrors, and parlor furniture are unharmed. The bureaus, closets with house linen, eatables, and wearables are all gone. This desk was much cut and pulled, but they could not force the lock. It is the only place locked which was not forced open. It had all my stationery which I had out here (not much). I lost nothing but a piece of cotton which I had forgotten and some little trashy things I left in my drawers. The bureau can be repaired and is not all defaced.[261]

She went on to say that they had taken her photographs and some of the blankets but left most of them "perfectly clean and precisely as we left them hanging over the foot of the beds." She concluded by saying she was "very busy putting things away and looking up things sent by General Breckinridge to the Wilsons and those taken away by Mrs. Beale. The trees and lawn are untouched; the servants are the greatest suffers."[262]

Three days later, on July 30, she provided additional details, saying, "General Jackson's letter, Mr. Van Buren's, and other prominent men's letters" were all safe, but some business papers and deeds were missing or torn while others were left unharmed. She went on to say, "Uncle Dick covered one of Blair's setting turkeys with a pile of brush just in the middle of the lawn, and strange to say, she was not much disturbed. She has hatched 6 turkeys and as many chickens, over which Blair was in a great glee; Grandma too. As to the chickens, 'they are *gamer* for being hatched by a turkey.' So with his dog Ned and these new pets Blair is quite consoled for his other losses."[263]

Elizabeth Blair Lee complained in early August that the "loss of five mules reduces our movements to the carriage horses. Even mother's riding horse is helping to get out the rye, which is all the feed left since the Rebs cleaned out the corn crib."[264] In another letter she mentioned "the empty Barn—lawn cut—Six thousand dollars will not cover all of Father's losses and would not now replace them."[265] But things were not all bad. She also noted that "one of the cows came back. She was hard to drive [by the Confederates] and broke a rope and got home at last. She is the *muley* cow so we have two cows now. All the hogs got back too."[266]

She also speculated that perhaps the Confederates had not been responsible for all the destruction and theft: "I think much of the robbing was done by others after the Rebs left. Flat irons and tubs are not things they are likely to take."[267] Her speculation may have been based on experience. About eight months earlier, her father had placed an ad in the *Evening Star* promising a $10 reward (equivalent to about $185 in 2014) for return of a female Pointer dog stolen from "Silver Spring."[268]

Writing in 1881, Early said that he had found Francis Preston Blair's house "in charge of some woman who fled on our approach." He went on to say that Blair's home had been abandoned and already plundered when he got there and posted a guard. He also said that he recovered most of the stolen property and gave it to a neighbor to return to Blair. He justified taking Blair's cattle: "His cattle, which were fit for beeves, were taken by my orders, as were the cattle of other citizens, it being necessary that my troops should be supplied with provisions from the country."[269] General Early failed to mention that his troops had ransacked Blair's papers and that some of the home's furniture and other contents had been damaged or destroyed, not to mention that all of the liquor had been consumed. At least the fields had been untouched.[270]

The Blairs were very fortunate that Early and Breckinridge had been as successful at protecting "Silver Spring" as they were. One local resident later reported that a colonel had ordered "Silver Spring" burned and said that "if he had his way he would not leave a Blair a shed to live under as the whole 'set' root and branch had done the South more harm than any other 'set of people.'"[271] Montgomery Blair, of course, had not been as fortunate as his father. His sister described his "Falkland" as "that blackened ruin on the hill before us."[272]

Although Francis Preston Blair's losses were slight in comparison to his son's, one loss was a statue that was near a pool by the spring. A Union artillery shell had broken a foot off the statue and reportedly killed a Confederate soldier who happened to be drinking from the pool when the shell hit. He had been buried near the pool.[273] In the late 1890s, while installing a hydraulic ram water system, Blair Lee came upon those remains or perhaps the remains of another dead Confederate. He had the body reburied and erected a monument bearing a plaque with the words: "Unknown Confederate Soldier Killed at the Spring by a Shell from Fort Stevens July 12, 1864."[274] The monument also included a niche containing a shell from a Parrott gun.

At least one other Confederate was also buried on Blair's estate. A Union report said the first Confederate killed by Union pickets fell and was buried near the house of Mrs. Martha Barnes, "who lives the upper end of Blair's place, [and] was at home all the time the rebels were in the neighborhood."[275]

Damage from the battle was not confined to the Blair property. As Elizabeth Blair Lee noted in one of her letters, "The battle was fought along the ridge from Mansions house, by the cousins Colclazers [immediately east of Georgia Avenue probably near Butternut Street], to Moorings [the Blair mansion still standing in Jesup Blair Park], up to Wilsons [farms on either side of Georgia Avenue north of Colesville Road]. They left their dead

The Blair family monument to a Confederate soldier killed near the spring on their "Silver Spring" estate, circa 1909–19. *Library of Congress.*

and wounded—not in our house as reported, but at Graves [store and Post Office] and that village."[276]

A July 18, 1864 dispatch to the *New York Times* published on July 22 provided an account of the post-battle situation in the entire area and said that "all kinds of vehicles have been in great demand" since the previous Friday "conveying strangers and the inhabitants to the scene of the recent conflict."[277]

The *Times* report went on to describe the battle area north of Fort Stevens, as seen on the Saturday after the battle:

> *To the right and left of the road, a short distance* [north] *from the fort, stand the chimney-stacks, all that remains of the residences of Messrs. Bell and Butt* [at approximately Sheridan Street, NW]. *Further on you come to the toll-gate, kept by a Mr. Fetman. One of our Colonels was wounded in the gate-house, which is pretty well perforated with balls. To the left of this the house of Mr. Thompson* [perhaps east of Piney Branch Road near Whittier Street, NW], *on Back Creek, was destroyed, it is thought by shells from Fort Stevens, as it was used by the*

rebels as cover for their sharpshooters. On the pike near the toll-gate, a large house, formerly used as a store, with a blacksmith's shop adjoining, was burnt by our own men, to prevent the rebels from making it a lodgment for their skirmishers. On still further, three houses—one on the right of the road, and two on the left—belonging to the McChestineys, were likewise burnt. Just above, the rebels built a barricade across the road with fence rails, and on the farm of Mr. Wilkins threw up earthworks and dug rifle-pits. The house of Mr. Wilkins, on the right, and back some distance from the road, is completely riddled with shot and shell. On one side over one hundred and twenty musket shots were counted, fired by our men in their advance. Seven or eight shell [sic] from the fort went right through, making some ugly looking holes. Its contents were either destroyed or carried off. Mr. Lay's house, said to have been a splendid mansion, to the left of the road, and nearly opposite Wilkins, was fired by the rebels, although some say it was from shells from our side. At all events, the family did not save even a change of clothing. A member of the Twenty-fifth New York Cavalry is buried on the roadside. At the corner of a corn field, near Mr. Lay's barn, thirteen rebel graves were counted.

SILVER SPRING

The next place of interest is Silver Spring, the residence of the Blairs, nine miles [sic] from Washington, used in the recent raid as the headquarters of Gens. Early and Breckinridge. Entering a gateway, a serpentine road through the woods brings you to the house of F.P. Blair, Sr., a rather fine-appearing mansion. There was apparently little evidence of the rebels to be seen here.

DEPREDATIONS

I looked in through one of the windows, and the furniture seemed to have been scarcely disturbed, but the man in charge of the place informed me that the rebels had done a great deal of damage to the furniture, besides carrying off many valuable relics and papers belonging to Mr. Blair. They also appropriated his cattle, five mules, one horse, and two Shetland ponies. The two ponies were sent back by Gen. Breckinridge after his retreat. Some old liquors, stores, etc., were taken for the benefit of Breckinridge's mess.[278]

The *Times* article also described the scene at the Sligo Post Office, which had served as the Confederate hospital:

REBEL SURGEONS

Leaving [the Blair "Silver Spring" mansion] *we went on to a rebel hospital camp, a mile or so further on where we met three rebel surgeons, who had in charge their wounded. We found them very agreeable in conversation, and readily gave us all the information they were at liberty to give. They were left behind on the retreat to take care of their own wounded. They had their own hospital stores, and, strange to say, a small barrel of genuine Confederate whiskey, direct from Richmond. Their uniforms were gray, of better material than is usually seen on rebel officers.*

THEIR OPINION OF THE RAID

Their losses in the fight they placed at 150. They were certain it would not exceed this number.

They conversed with great frankness and laughed at the excitement they had created in Washington. They said this was their third annual visit, and they should surely come back again in '65. It was an expedition sent expressly to replenish the exhausted stores of their army, and that they had no intention of taking Washington but only to give us a big scare, which they flattered themselves they had accomplished. As regards the number of men comprising their force they were silent but enough was gleaned to believe that no more than 15,000 crossed the Potomac and it is doubtful if there were as many.

THEY ARE FAVORITES WITH THE LADIES

There were many visitors to see the surgeons, and quite a large number of ladies, who expressed themselves delighted with their society. They begged buttons from their coats as keepsakes, giving them some trifling article in return as mementos of their visit. Delicacies were brought to them, and every attention is paid to their wants. Instead of being treated as prisoners they were feted as conquerors. Surgeon Covert, the surgeon in charge, said to me, "These ladies are in love with us dirty Confeds and have treated us splendidly." I thought so too, and that I wouldn't mind being myself a prisoner under such favorable circumstances...

These surgeons with five men left to assist the wounded did not appear to have been paroled, nor considered to be in custody, up to the time of my visit. Nothing prevented them from going into Washington if they desired to do so, and Surgeon Covert said, in a joking way, he thought he would take his bag and go in and stop at Willard's [Willard's hotel in downtown Washington] *that night. On Saturday, the day of our visit, no passes were required; at least none were demanded, and consequently the road was clear for everyone, so nothing would have prevented the Surgeon from carrying out his joke, had he desired to do so.*[279]

It should not have been surprising that the surgeons and their assistants were not "considered to be in custody." According to Article 53 of General Orders No. 100 as promulgated by President Lincoln on April 24, 1863, to provide rules of conduct for the army, "The enemy's chaplains, officers of the medical staff, apothecaries, hospital nurses and servants, if they fall into the hands of the American Army, are not prisoners of war, unless the commander has reasons to retain them."[280] Apparently, no commander ordered them held as prisoners, and surgeons left at Silver Spring were free to do as they wished.

The retreating Confederates had plundered the countryside. The *New York Times* reported in a dispatch dated July 14 that "the Confederate forces commenced to leave early yesterday morning, carrying away with them their immense plunder. Many of those who came on foot will go back mounted, as they have cleared out all the stables where they have been marauding." Someone who witnessed the retreating Confederates pass through Rockville stated that the Rebel rear guard had passed through the town "driving before them several thousand head of cattle and a large number of horses" but that "they did not appear to have many prisoners." The *Times* summarized that "the rebels have suffered little loss compared with the immense amount of plunder they successfully carried away." The invasion only "seems to have culminated in plundering the richest counties in Maryland and cutting railroads between Washington and the North."[281]

Reports of stolen horses were widespread. For example, the Rebels took four valuable horses from a pasture near Beltsville. Another report had two horses stolen near Bladensburg, but "several old 'bags of bones' [were] left in their places."[282]

The *Evening Star* suggested on July 14 that plunder rather than capture of Washington had been the Rebels' real goal. The story centered on wounded Confederates who had been taken from the hospital tents at the Sligo Post Office to Lincoln Hospital after the battle. The wounded said that "they made this show on our front to draw off attention while they cleaned out 'My Maryland,' and [they] are quite jubilant that they were so successful, their cavalry having scoured all that portion of Maryland west of the Railroad [from Washington to Baltimore], which they completely stripped of livestock, &c., while the infantry kept the attention of our forces near

Fort Stevens…[They had] moved over into Maryland on a plundering raid and with the hope of drawing off Grant from Richmond." The wounded Confederates also told the *Evening Star* that about 200 Marylanders had joined their army in Frederick County and another 1,500 had joined in the Baltimore area.[283]

Two days later, the *Evening Star* had a different interpretation: the Confederate raid had been a failure. They had been "foiled in their expectation of seizing Washington by surprise." Furthermore, "it is doubtful the rebel invasionists will make 'day wages' by their raid, as, with their forced marches, they will break down quite as many horses as they stole, and the cattle they drove away will be devoured in provisioning the rebel raiders on their way to Richmond. A few of the thieving raiders may be the better for the trip to the extent of some pocket money stolen from individuals, but we doubt if Jeff. Davis will not be loser rather than gainer by the expedition."[284]

Failure or not, Silver Spring area residents had not fared well. Their fields had been trampled and their livestock stolen. The Confederates had occupied most of the houses north of Fort Stevens as far north as Woodside and Woodside Park and beyond. Elizabeth Blair Lee summarized the situation for her husband:

> *Not a day passes that a new case of suffering does not come to light. I do not know a single poor man in this neighborhood whose house, garden, horse, cow, and pigs have not all been taken. Even Bill Gittlings, who has been always so hot Secesh, was "cleaned out," while Riggs, Wilson, Birch* [farm just east of the Wilson farm north of Colesville Road], *Beale, and others have had only their hay forage and the eatables grown by their families eaten. Riggs lost one ox, but all his fine blooded cattle was untouched. Our hay was taken to Wilsons and fed to Secesh Headquarters horses. No poor man escaped. Mrs. Jones* [a domestic who lived near the Blairs] *had nothing left in her house but her bedstead and cupboard. Mrs. Cook* [Martha Byrnes Cook, gardener Ned Byrnes' mother, who lived nearby] *and everybody of that class fared alike, no matter what their politics. This, added to the drought, makes me look forward to winter with real anxiety for these poor people.*[285]

Whether in a panic or by a simple coincidence, George Washington Riggs had sold his estate by the time Elizabeth Blair Lee wrote her letter. On July 21, just a little more than a week after Early's Confederates had left the area, he sold the property for $22,000, which is equivalent to about $319,000 in 2014.[286]

On August 18, Elizabeth Lee wrote again to her husband: "Our old Shoemaker told Blair and Ned that he told them (Secesh) that they would never get in Washington and that they had best leave Mr. Blair's house since some people out here would need him for bread to eat. This old man's boldness saved him. General Early is said to have told him that the women and old men of Maryland were the bravest Union people he had ever yet met. Maryland women as a general thing gave the Secesh Army a cold welcome."[287]

The *Washington Chronicle* had a somewhat different take on the extent to which the Confederates had left the population destitute: "The tenor of advices from Montgomery County is to the effect that the rebels did not make an indiscriminate sweep of horses and cattle, but that in many cases they levied upon property somewhat in respect to the means of the possessors to contribute."[288]

The *New York Times* also noted plundering in the Silver Spring area: "The dwelling of Marshall Bonifant [near the current Silver Spring International Middle School, the former Montgomery Blair High School] was ransacked from cellar to garret, and everything available was carried off. In several of the houses the Confederates left notices in books, stating that the reason they destroyed property was in retaliation for the destruction of property in Virginia."[289]

Noah Brooks, correspondent of the *Sacramento Union*, said he "found traces of rebel occupation five or six miles from Washington [i.e., the Silver Spring area, five or six miles north of the city boundary at today's Florida Avenue], where houses had been held by the invaders, the rightful owners thereof having incontinently fled at the approach of the enemy. Horses had been picketed in the orchards; fences were torn down and used for firewood, and books, letters and women's wearing-apparel were scattered about the grounds, showing that the raiders had made the best use of their time in looting houses where they had been quartered." He went on to say that "in one comfortable family mansion, now in a sad state of wreck, we found such disorder as might have reigned if a wild Western cyclone had swept through the building. Furniture was smashed, crockery broken, and even a handsome piano was split up in the very wantonness of destruction. Obscene drawings covered the walls, and one inscription, scrawled with charcoal over the place where the piano had stood, read, 'Fifty thousand Virginian homes have been devastated in like manner.'"[290]

Not all the local houses were ransacked or destroyed. The Wilsons' homes were spared. Richard T. Wilson, whose father had been killed in the 1862 pig-stealing incident, was a Confederate sympathizer and was honored to have Confederate general and former U.S. vice president John C. Breckinridge in his home. In fact, his wife, Laura, prepared a feast for their guests. The hospitality undoubtedly spared his home, "Woodside" (now 8818 First Avenue), and the home of his brother John C. Wilson, who lived in the home he inherited from his murdered father, Thomas Noble Wilson. Unlike his brother, John C. Wilson opposed secession, perhaps influenced by his wife, Selina, whose parents were Union sympathizers.[291] Regardless, Early issued a "Special Order" stating, "All officers & men of the C.S.A. are forbidden to take from Mr. J.C.D. Wilson his horses, or a pair of horses belonging to Mr. Blair." Nevertheless, John C. Wilson took the precaution of burying his silver and other items to keep them from Confederate looters. Silver belonging to Montgomery Blair was also buried for safekeeping. His silver was buried on Richard T. Wilson's farm and returned to him by Laura Wilson.[292]

Richard T. Wilson's hospitality had not protected his home or his brother's home from Union shelling. An unexploded cannonball was found in the 1920s at the base of a tree near Richard T. Wilson's home. A live ten-inch Parrott shell was discovered during excavation for an addition to the back of a later neighboring home at 1504 Noyes Drive. An army team from Fort McNair recovered and detonated the shell. In Woodside Park, the damage to two of John C. Wilson's outbuildings and firing into Raymond Burche's field have already been noted. Richard T. Wilson filed a damage claim and was eventually paid $1,455 (more than $35,000 in 2014 dollars) by the federal government.[293]

The businesses at the Sligo intersection of Georgia Avenue and Colesville Road also had not fared well. Lewis Graves' dry goods store and Rayney's store, or both, were sacked. Barnes' Tavern farther south was also looted.

Northeast of Sligo, Dr. Condict's house high on a hill overlooking Sligo Creek west of Colesville Road had been used as a Confederate observation post. The Condict property also was likely the site of "two small cavalry camps to the eastward, near the Sligo [Creek], formed apparently as a rendezvous for roving bands of cavalry in search for horses, &c, for observation on the extreme left."[294] Fortunately for Dr. Condict, his house wasn't particularly damaged. Canister shot left by the Confederates was found in the vicinity of the house. A dismembered human femur said by the state coroner's office to be "old" and likely from a Civil War casualty was also found when the telephone pole between 1205 and 1209 Edgevale Road in Woodside Forest was replaced in the late 2000s or early 2010s. There was speculation that the bone came with fill dirt taken from downtown Silver Spring when the houses were constructed in 1966.[295]

Among the items found by the Union troops in their search of the battlefield and the area previously held by the Confederates was a book by Lord Byron that had been stolen from a local resident's house by someone in Early's army. On the flyleaf was inscribed: "Now Uncle Abe, you had better be quiet the balance of your administration. We only came near your town this time to show you what we can do, but if you go on in your mad career we will come again soon, and then you had better stand under.—Yours, respectfully, The Worst Rebel You Ever Saw."[296]

Other messages left by the Confederates were directed at private citizens. The *Evening Star* reported that "Ed Tyler, a son of Major Tyler, formerly of the U.S. Marines, was with the rebels in front of Fort Stevens and left a letter at the house of Mr. Fenwick [west of Georgia Avenue just north of Colesville Road], beyond Blair's, in which he stated that he understood that Marshal Lamont [*sic*] [probably U.S. marshal for the District of Columbia and later Lincoln biographer Ward Hill Lamon] lived in his father's house, (F street, near 7th,) and he would like very much to have the pleasure of burning it down."[297]

The aggressiveness of the Union search of the area previously occupied by Early's army led to many complaints. One of the first to complain, and certainly the most prominent, was Postmaster General Montgomery Blair. His complaint, however, was not about the behavior of the Union army after Early left. Indeed, the army had gone out of its way to post guards to protect his father's "Silver Spring" from further damage. Instead, his complaint was about the army's failure to prevent the invasion itself and the accompanying destruction of his "Falkland." According to his sister Elizabeth Blair Lee, Montgomery Blair was met at the steps of his burned "Falkland" by Richard Cutts, aide-de-camp to Army chief of staff Halleck, on the morning on July 13, shortly after Early had withdrawn his troops. When Cutts expressed his sorrow about the destruction of Blair's house, Blair told him, "I am not conscious of a sensation about the house. My every feeling is swallowed up by indignation at the imbecility and treason of those men to whom this Capitol has been a peculiar charge and by whom it has been exposed to insult."[298]

This remark was reported by Cutts and was not well received by the army command. That same day, Halleck wrote to Secretary of War Stanton:

> *Sir: I deem it my duty to bring to your notice the following facts: I am informed by an officer of rank and standing in the military service that the Hon. M. Blair, Postmaster-General, in speaking of the burning of his house in Maryland, this morning, said, in effect, that "the officers in*

command about Washington are poltroons [lazy or spiritless cowards], *that there were not more than five hundred rebels on the Silver Spring road, and we had a million of men in arms; that it was a disgrace; that General Wallace was in comparison with them far better, as he would at least fight."*

As there have been for the last few days a large number of officers on duty in and about Washington who have devoted their time and energies night and day, and have periled their lives in support of the Government, it is due to them, as well as to the War Department, that it should be known whether such wholesale denouncement and accusation by a member of the Cabinet receives the sanction and approbation of the President of the United States. If so, the names of the officers accused should be stricken from the rolls of the Army; if not, it is due to the honor of the accused that the slanderer should be dismissed from the Cabinet.[299]

Secretary Stanton, with whom Blair had an ongoing feud (Blair thought Stanton was "a great scoundrel" who "would cut the President's throat if he could"),[300] sent Halleck's complaint to Lincoln. Lincoln replied:

Your note of to-day, inclosing Gen. Halleck's letter of yesterday, relative to offensive remarks supposed to have been made by the Post-Master-General concerning the Military officers on duty about Washington, is received. The General's letter, in substance demands of me that if I approve the remarks, I shall strike the names of those officers from the rolls; and that if I do not approve them, the Post-Master-General shall be dismissed from the Cabinet. Whether the remarks were really made I do not know; nor do I suppose such knowledge is necessary to a correct response. If they were made I do not approve them; and yet, under the circumstances, I would not dismiss a member of the Cabinet therefor. I do not consider what may have been hastily said in a moment of vexation at so severe a loss is sufficient ground for so grave a step. Besides this, truth is generally the best vindication against slander. I propose continuing to be myself the judge as to when a member of the Cabinet shall be dismissed.[301]

At the next cabinet meeting, Lincoln said he would be the judge of who to retain and who to remove from the cabinet and that he didn't want any of the cabinet members trying to have others removed either by public statements or in private.[302]

As the days passed, Blair cooled down about the loss of his house. On August 10, he sent a letter rebuking General Butler for burning the home near Fredericksburg of Confederate secretary of war James Seddon in retaliation for the burning of "Falkland." He concluded by saying:

> *If we allow the military to invade the rights of private property on any other grounds than those recognized by civilized warfare, there will soon cease to be any security whatever for the rights of civilians on either side. The tendency of such measures is to involve our country in all the horrors of the Wars of the Fronde, of the petty Princes and Brigands of Italy, of the Guerillas of Spain, which made the plunder of the peaceful citizens' homes, highway robbery and assassination, the concomitants of the war. No man, I know, would appreciate such results more than myself, and there are no talents on which I would sooner rely than yours to prevent it, if you had proper support.*[303]

Blair also declined offered financial help from friends to rebuild, asking, "Could I consent to have my house rebuilt by friends, whilst my neighbor a poor old blacksmith is unrelieved[?]."[304]

Despite his mellowing, Blair's long-standing inability to get along with other cabinet members and continuing impolitic public statements took their toll on Lincoln's patience. The cabinet feud got to the point that Stanton refused to attend cabinet meetings if Blair attended. Lincoln was also told that he would lose thousands of votes in the upcoming election if Blair remained postmaster general, but if Blair resigned, he would pick up radical support and John C. Fremont would drop his candidacy. Lincoln ultimately requested and then accepted Blair's resignation in September, about two months after Blair's complaint about the army.[305]

Montgomery Blair was not the only person in the Blair family who continued to suffer at least some fallout from Early's invasion. The battleground and "Silver Spring" continued to be popular local tourist destinations. Elizabeth Blair Lee and, presumably, other family members found this to be a nuisance as late as August 21, almost six weeks after the battle. "There are sometimes 15 or 16 hacks full of people at the Spring [the spring now in Acorn Park] and wandering all over the place to see what the Rebs wrote and did here and to see the Rebel graves. We do not notice now the coming of carriages any more than we do at No 4 [their home, now "Blair House" on Pennsylvania Avenue across from the Eisenhower Executive Office Building]. We are civil but we do not receive these visitors. Our nearness to the city makes it something like the Mt. Vernon visitors."[306]

There were also complaints of a different nature. Lord Lyons complained to Secretary of State Seward, whose son had been wounded in actions against Early's troops, about water torture of British subjects who allegedly had been forced into the Union army and then accused of desertion. He claimed water cannons were being used "for the purpose of extorting, by the infliction of bodily pain, confessions from persons suspected of being deserters." The State Department dismissed the complaints and said cold showers were pleasant in the hot summer. Meanwhile, the British consulate in New York told Lyons that British subjects accused of desertion from the Union army were being hung by their thumbs until they confessed.[307]

There were also complaints that the army had done little to stop Early as he retreated and destroy his army. Despite Lincoln's urging, Union forces had made only a halfhearted attempt to catch up with Early's retreating forces. According to *Sacramento Union* correspondent Noah Brooks, who spoke to Lincoln about it and "learned from his own lips," Lincoln had been more worried that the Confederates would escape than that they would capture Washington. Lincoln "said that General Halleck's manifest desire to avoid taking any responsibility without the immediate sanction of General Grant was the main reason why the rebels, having threatened Washington and sacked the peaceful farms and villages of Maryland, got off scatheless… [Lincoln] was 'agonized' (as he said) over the evident failure of all attempts at pursuit."[308]

As time went on, there were continuing small raids farther north in Montgomery County. For example, on October 7, 1864, Walter Bowie and other raiders under the command of the "Gray Ghost," Colonel John S. Mosby, robbed a general store in Sandy Spring. The Quakers of Sandy Spring went after them and killed Bowie in the Battle of Rickets Run, near the current Redland Road and Somerville Drive intersection.[309] Union troops occupied lower Montgomery County for the remainder of the war. As the war was ending in May 1865, a report noted that Major General John A. Logan, commanding the Army of Tennessee, was camped near Silver Spring, and his two corps were camped nearby on Fourteenth Street extended.[310]

On May 31, 1865, the last reported event in Silver Spring involving the army took place. It was a "strawberry party" honoring Major General Francis Preston (Frank) Blair Jr. and the staff officers of the Seventeenth Corps held by his brother Montgomery Blair at his presumably now rebuilt "Falkland" in Silver Spring.[311]

Chapter 12

A FINAL ROLE FOR A
SILVER SPRING RESIDENT

Although peace returned to Silver Spring after Early's raid and homes and farms were repaired, the war continued. Silver Spring resident Francis Preston Blair continued to have a role. In the five months after the Confederates had occupied and sacked his home and had most likely been responsible for burning the home of his son, Blair developed a plan to end the war. He proposed to go to Richmond to speak with his longtime friend Confederate president Jefferson Davis about ending the war. The idea was that the two armies would stop fighting each other and instead join forces to uphold the Monroe Doctrine by invading Mexico and driving out the French-installed puppet emperor Maximilian I. Lincoln was agreeable to this effort but wanted Blair to wait until after Savannah fell to General Sherman, which happened on November 21, 1864. About two weeks after receiving permission to go to Richmond from both Lincoln (on December 28) and Davis (on December 30), Blair traveled as a private citizen, not an official emissary, to Richmond. He met privately with Davis on January 12, 1865. At the conclusion of the long meeting, Davis gave Blair a letter addressed to Blair but to be shown to Lincoln, in which he said he was ready to enter into peace negotiations and would send or receive commissioners, ministers or agents "with a view to secure peace to **the two countries** [emphasis added]."[312]

Blair returned to Washington and showed Davis' letter to Lincoln. On January 18, Lincoln responded with a letter addressed to Blair for Davis stating that he was ready to talk to "any agent whom he or any other influential person now resisting the national authority may informally send to me with the view of securing peace to the people of **our one common country** [emphasis added]."[313]

Blair shuttled back to Richmond with Lincoln's letter and again met with Davis on January 21. He then returned to Washington. Meanwhile, word of Blair's effort had spread in Washington. Those opposed to any negotiations with the Confederacy pressed for quick passage of the Thirteenth Amendment, which would abolish slavery and was supported by Lincoln. They thought adoption of the amendment would be a poison pill for the Confederacy.[314]

Davis named three commissioners to go to Washington: Confederate vice president Alexander H. Stephens, who had advocated ending the war since 1863; Confederate assistant secretary of war John A. Campbell, who had worked to prevent the outbreak of the war and by late 1864 was working to end it; and Robert M.T. Hunter, who represented Virginia in the Confederate Senate. They were to have an "informal conference" with Lincoln. They reached Union lines on January 29 but were not permitted to cross pending instructions from Washington. Those instructions came the next day, but before the instructions arrived, the commissioners applied directly to General Grant to cross into Union-held territory. He had them admitted and taken to his headquarters. After further confusion, on February 1, Grant suggested to Lincoln that Lincoln should receive the commissioners, saying that his failure to do so would have unfortunate results. Meanwhile, Congress had passed the Thirteenth Amendment and sent it to the states for ratification. The commissioners were so informed.[315]

Even congressional passage of a constitutional amendment to abolish slavery and Lincoln's refusal to acknowledge the Confederate commissioners as having any official role did not scuttle the peace efforts that had resulted from Blair's initiative. Arrangements were made for a meeting on a Union navy ship anchored off Fort Monroe. On February 3, 1865, Lincoln and Secretary of State Seward met for four hours with the Confederate commissioners in what came to be known as the Hampton Roads Conference. By mutual agreement, no written notes were kept, but after the war, Stephens said that Lincoln started the meeting by saying that whatever Blair had said was "on his own accord and without authority from me." Both sides rejected Blair's idea of forming a joint army to drive Maximilian out of Mexico. Lincoln required a pledge of ultimate restoration of the Union as a precondition to any end of hostilities. The only positive result of the meeting was a resumption of prisoner exchanges.[316] Lincoln agreed to release Vice President Stephens' nephew, and the Confederates agreed to release a Union official; Lincoln also agreed to recommend that Grant set up a method for prisoner exchanges. Grant did start exchanging prisoners, but the war continued.[317]

The end came relatively soon. Union troops entered Richmond on April 3, 1865. Lee surrendered the Army of Northern Virginia to Grant at Appomattox six days later. Various small units surrendered through May and into June. The Confederate navy held out longer. All hostilities finally ceased on November 6, 1865, when the captain of the CSS *Shenandoah* surrendered his ship to HMS *Donegal* in the River Mersey at Liverpool, the unofficial home of the Confederate fleet. The *Shenandoah* had sailed all the way from Alaska to surrender there. The Royal Navy subsequently turned the ship over to the U.S. government.

President Andrew Johnson formally declared the war over on August 20, 1866.

Chapter 13

MEMORIALS TO THE FALLEN AND THE WAR'S FINAL SILVER SPRING CASUALTY

After the war ended, its effects lingered in the hearts and minds of local residents. In 1874, ten years after Early's raid, Reverend James B. Avirett, the pastor of Grace Church and a former Confederate soldier, led an effort to move the bodies of seventeen Confederates buried on the Osborn farm near Fort Stevens to the Grace Church cemetery. Reportedly, there were three officers and fourteen privates. All were said to be unknown except for Private James B. Bland, "a member of the 62d Virginia mounted infantry, of Imboden's brigade,"[318] which was also sometimes known as the Eighteenth Mounted Partisans. Private Bland had enlisted in Pendleton County, Virginia (now West Virginia), on September 4, 1862. He is listed in Confederate records as having been wounded on July 11, 1864, in Washington, D.C., and dying the following day.[319]

On December 8, 1874, the seventeen bodies were placed in "six plain coffins" and taken to Grace Church for a ceremonial reburial held three days later. About three hundred people attended. "Quite a large number" had gathered at Ninth Street and Pennsylvania Avenue in Washington and taken carriages to the church. Many others came from "Rockville and the country round about." A grave large enough for all six coffins had been dug in an enclosure in front of the church, which faced Georgia Avenue north of the cemetery. Following a church service with scripture reading, hymns and prayers, a wreath was placed on each coffin. Then each was lowered into the grave. Private Bland's coffin was placed at the north end of the row so his friends and relatives could find him.[320] According to the Grace Church history, which may be of doubtful accuracy given the exhumed bodies had been buried for ten years, "Those who viewed the bodies, before burial, told that they were impressed by the extreme youth of the poor lads; none looked as old as twenty, and all seemed barely in their teens."[321]

Dr. Alexander Y.P. Garnett of Washington, who had been Jefferson Davis' physician during the war, whose property had been the first to be confiscated in Washington as belonging to an enemy alien[322] and who was later president of the American Medical Association, then made an hour-long oration. He spoke of the causes of the war and justified the South's action. According to the *Evening Star*, "He once alluded to the willingness of the south to take up arms to defend their homes from invasion, when a voice in the crowd said, 'And we are still willing to do it, Dr.' He alluded to the south as 'our people' and Jeff Davis as 'our President.'"[323] Clearly, the wounds of the war had not yet been bound up in Silver Spring.

Indeed, in 1896, thirty-one years after the war's end, the bitterness of the period immediately after the war was the root cause of the war's last damage in Silver Spring. When Grace Church caught fire and burned to the ground, no water was readily available to put it out because of postwar ill feelings.

The events leading to the destruction of the church building began two years after the end of the war but were a direct result of the war. In 1867, the Grace Church vestry bought additional land behind the original church lot for $200 ($5,450 in 2014 dollars) from John C. Wilson to build a rectory but soon backed out of the deal and had its $200 returned. The vestry reportedly took this action because John C. Wilson and his wife had been Union sympathizers during the war. This was not an amiable transaction. As the published church history put it, "When the war was over, those who had been Unionists were treated like lepers by the majority of the people on the plantations, even the ministers and their families taking sides. This together with the demands made upon him to refund the $200 plus 6 percent interest, and take back his lot, caused that branch of the Wilson family to withdraw from the church."[324]

The vestry purchased a larger lot across Georgia Avenue from John C. Wilson's brother Richard, who had inherited the portion of Thomas Noble Wilson's farm west of Georgia Avenue after his father was killed in the 1862 pig-stealing incident.[325] The price was $637.50 ($10,400 in 2014 dollars). Richard Wilson was an acceptable seller. He had volunteered his home to Confederate major general (and former U.S. vice president) John C. Breckinridge for use as a headquarters for himself and his staff officers during Early's raid in 1864 and treated them to a banquet. The rectory was subsequently built on the lot across the road from the church rather than behind the church.

Almost thirty years later, on June 6, 1896, the church building caught fire during choir practice when a singer accidentally knocked over a kerosene light while slapping at a moth.

> *A moth flew in the open window and Mrs. Woodward hit at it, thereby upsetting the lighted lamp. The kerosene flew over everything including herself. She was enveloped in flames immediately. Mr. Birgfeld frantically tore down the choir curtain, wrapped it around the burning woman, and then threw her to the floor and rolled her down the aisle to extinguish the flames. His quick action saved her life. She was horribly burned, however, and, to add to her discomfort, someone put raw cotton on the burns before she arrived at the hospital in Washington. After a long illness she recovered.*
>
> *People arrived at the scene of the tragedy as speedily as was possible in those days, when horses or one's own feet were the only means of transportation. A bucket brigade was formed from the well at the rectory across the street, but nothing could be done to save the building. In an hour it was a smouldering ruin, burned to the ground.*
>
> *The Brightwood Fire Department heard of the fire and came as far as the District Line, but seeing the trouble was in Maryland, returned to its headquarters, for the fire was out of its jurisdiction...However they could have done nothing even if they had arrived, for there was no water available except from the rectory pump across the road.*[326]

Had the vestry in 1867 not been prejudiced against John C. Wilson and his pro-Union views, Mrs. Woodward would still have been injured in the fire, but the rectory and its well would have been adjacent to the church and the building might have been saved even without the reluctant firefighters from Brightwood.

Perhaps the unfortunate fire ultimately contributed to a degree of reconciliation concerning the Civil War. That might not have been evident when a committee of Confederate veterans was formed before the fire in 1895 to build a monument to their seventeen fallen comrades buried at Grace Church, but it was evident by the end of the monument's dedication ceremony on November 14, 1896, five months after the fire.

The monument's creation and dedication began as a Confederate Veterans Association effort. Possibly in reaction to news that a trolley line was to be built along the road in front of Grace Church near the line of

The Confederate monument at Grace Church cemetery, dedicated on November 14, 1896. "To the Memory of Seventeen Unknown Confederate Dead Who Fell in Front of Washington, D.C. July 12, 1864. By Their Comrades." *Photo by the author.*

graves, Confederate veterans' "camps" in Washington and Rockville decided to move the graves and erect a Confederate monument to honor the fallen soldiers. The proposed monument was said by the *Evening Star* to be the first Civil War monument in Montgomery County.[327]

After the Confederate veterans raised the necessary money, the graves were moved from in front of the church to what is now the corner of Georgia Avenue and Grace Church Road. A new nine-foot-high granite monument was erected. On a cold Saturday afternoon, a large crowd, including large contingents of Confederate veterans from both Rockville and Washington, attended the dedication ceremony. Many of the Washingtonians had taken the 12:50 p.m. train from Washington to the B&O's Woodside Station, which was only a few blocks from the church. After band music, opening remarks about the creation of the monument and a prayer, Robert E. Lee's General Orders No. 9—his farewell address to the Army of Northern Virginia—was read. "The Bivouac of the Dead," a poem by Theodore O'Hara, was then recited by three Woodside girls. This was followed by the reading of a letter from Brigadier General William R. Cox, who had commanded the seventeen fallen soldiers' unit during the war. Then came the oration. This time, the orator was Judge Samuel S. Blackwell, the third auditor of the Treasury. Judge Blackwell had been a colonel in the Confederate army and was active in the Confederate Veterans Association. His message was very different from that of twenty-two years before. He "remarked on the almost total obliteration of sectional lines and said that both North and South alike should now stand for the perpetuation of patriotism and the flag." Then "Mr. Paul Jones, a well-known citizen of Washington, whose father died fighting for the Union, arose and said that as a member of the Loyal Legion [a Union officers' veteran association] he claimed the privilege of recognizing the valor of the Confederate soldiers by laying at the foot of the monument a large bunch of white chrysanthemums."[328]

Clearly, if the healing in Silver Spring from the Civil War was not yet complete, it was well underway.

***

A mystery remains surrounding the seventeen Confederate soldiers buried at the Grace Church cemetery. Who are they? In 1874, the *Evening Star* reported that only one, Private James B. Bland, was known. Twenty-two years later, the *Evening Star* said that only two were known, and Private Bland was not one of them. The paper's 1896 story identified two brothers, Captain Butt and Lieutenant Butt of Augusta, Georgia, as the only known soldiers buried by the new monument. In a story almost too good to be true, the *Star* said, "Both were fatally wounded in the engagement. 'How's my brother?' asked one of them of the surgeon who was trying to save his life. 'Your brother is dead' [was the response]. 'And in thirty minutes I, too, shall be dead, the last of five brothers who have given their lives to the cause.' He died just an half hour later."[329]

Was it true? Confederate records list Privates (not a captain and a lieutenant) Daniel and Sim Butts (not Butt), both of Company H of the Fourth Georgia Infantry and both of Baldwin County, Georgia, as having been killed in Washington, D.C., in July 1864.[330] But Sim Butts is said to have been killed on July 12, and Daniel Butts is said to have been killed a day later. A further inconsistency is that Baldwin County is about ninety miles west of Augusta.

So was there even a germ of truth in the *Star*'s story? And what of Private Bland? Perhaps he had been buried in front of the church but forgotten in the twenty-two years before the bodies were moved to the corner with the new monument. Perhaps Privates Daniel and Sim Butts were somehow identified between 1874 and 1896, or perhaps the *Star*'s reporter in 1896 simply heard and repeated or embellished a good story. Although all agree that seventeen fallen Confederates are buried in the Grace Church cemetery, we may never know who even some of them are. But we do know that the hostility and bitterness that led to their deaths and many others have passed.

HOW MANY TROOPS DID EARLY HAVE AT SILVER SPRING?

The total number of troops under Early's command in Silver Spring was, and still is, open to debate. As the *Evening Star* put it on July 11, 1864, "Reports concerning the numbers and purpose of the rebel invading forces are confusing and conflicting."[331] Contemporary estimates and speculation varied widely, and the participants had various motives at various times to either underestimate or overestimate Early's strength. Early himself, for example, benefited at the time from making the Union defenders believe he had a very strong force, but after the war, his reputation was best served by claiming only a small force, which would justify his reluctance to press his attack on Washington.

A story in the *Evening Star* noted "the opinion entertained by many around us that the rebel force is not of weight sufficient to undertake a serious attack upon the fortifications of Washington, and that it is not their purpose to do so." However, the story went on to quote an unnamed person claimed to be "a source of great intelligence and reliability, one that on repeated occasions had the earliest and most accurate information," as saying that "the rebel army marched down the Valley 45,000 strong" and that its purpose was "an attempt at the capture of Washington by a surprise."[332]

The *National Intelligencer* said, "The number of the enemy's force at this point, or at any other, was utterly unknown to our military authorities, but it has been subsequently developed that at this locality [in front of Fort Stevens] it never much exceeded five or six hundred men,"[333] which seems ridiculously low as an estimate of all of Early's troops in the Silver Spring area but conceivably could be reasonable as an estimate of only those who actively skirmished in front of the fort.

A Confederate soldier who served under Early later supported the notion that the force was not large but still well above five to six hundred, putting the number at ten thousand.[334]

Four days after the battle was over, Major General Halleck, chief of staff, noted that estimates of Early's strength ranged from thirty to forty thousand. He also said, "The mass of evidence would make it a little less than the former number. Their loss at Monocacy and near Silver Spring was considerable, but they say they have made it up by volunteers, and conscripts."[335]

A Union prisoner taken with the Confederate column toward Fort Stevens later said that the force was "about 40,000 rebels."[336]

Union major general McCook estimated the strength of the advancing Confederate army at thirty thousand, composed of twenty-two thousand infantry, seven thousand cavalry and one thousand artillery.[337]

The brigadier in command of the Veteran Reserve Corps told L.E. Chittenden, the register of the Treasury, that he had heard Monday morning (July 11) from three independent sources that Early had over twenty thousand infantry, forty guns (artillery) and about six thousand cavalry, although some of them had gone around Baltimore to the Gunpowder River and others were between Washington and Baltimore.[338]

A July 21, 1864 post-battle "examination of the ground lately occupied by the rebels" drafted by E. Hergesheimer of the U.S. Coast Survey and Lieutenant J.H. Oberteuiffer Jr., an acting assistant adjutant general, provides additional support for the thirty thousand estimate:

> *Mrs.* [Martha] *Barnes, who lives at the upper end of Blair's place* [at Sligo], *was at home all the time the rebels were in the neighborhood. The first rebel killed by our pickets fell and was buried near her house. The rebels bivouacked around her house. She frequently heard their conversation, and from what she heard says their force was 30,000, and that their purpose was to make an attack early on Tuesday morning* [July 12].[339]

In a summary report, Major General Barnard, chief engineer, who was at Fort Reno, based his estimates on observations of dust being kicked up on Veirs Mill Road throughout the day on Monday, July 11. He said, "No very definite statement of actual numbers was obtained, but it is certain that, besides the 1,500 cavalry which approached Tennallytown, on the Rockville road, and the cavalry which encamped at Silver Spring, very heavy bodies of infantry came up on the Seventh-street road, bivouacking from Silver Spring to Batchelor's two miles distant. Twenty pieces of artillery are known to have been brought up to Silver Spring and five pieces were with McCausland's command [on Old Georgetown Road from Rockville toward Tenleytown]." He went on to say that the people along the Confederates' route confirmed his observations that "the columns were passing given points, both in advance and retreat, [for] a duration of nearly twelve hours."[340]

Early weighed in to the debate, writing in 1881:

The force of infantry that I moved on Washington did not...exceed 8,000 muskets, if it reached that number. In the three battalions of artillery I had nine batteries, neither of which had more than four field-pieces, and some of them had not that many. Besides these there were one or two battalions of horse artillery with the cavalry, the entire number of field-pieces in all the artillery not exceeding 40...

Some idea of my strength at the time of the advance on Washington may be formed from the return for the 31ˢᵗ of August, 1864 given by Col Taylor in his book, page 178. This, I presume is the earliest return on file with the Archives Office after I was detached, and it is as follows:

Breckinridge's division (total effectives)	*2,104*
Rodes' division (total effectives)	*3,013*
Gordon's division (total effectives)	*2,544*
Ramseur's division (total effectives)	*1,909*
Aggregate	*9,570*

The strength of the cavalry and artillery is not given, but both could not have exceeded 3,000. By this time all the stragglers had rejoined me, and some of those wounded in the campaign from the Wilderness had returned to their regiments.[341]

Early also suggested that Union army sources so overestimated his strength because he and his soldiers spread false information:

It was a very poor Confederate soldier who would acknowledge to citizens of the enemy's country through which he was marching the weakness of the army to which he belonged or any doubt of the success of the expedition. I recollect very well an incident which occurred with myself on that morning

[Monday, July 11]. *As I was riding in rear of my cavalry advance I got some distance ahead of my infantry column, and, seeing a shady grove by the roadside, with a neat house in it, I halted to rest under the shade of the trees while waiting for my infantry. The gentleman of the house came out to speak to me, and I soon found a sympathizer with our cause in him. Finding this, I asked him about the character and strength of the works around Washington, and he said that they were not very strong, as they were nothing but "earth-works." I then asked him about the strength of the troops inside of those works, and he stated that there was not a large force in them—not more, he thought, than 20,000 men. Knowing that earthworks in the then state of the science of war were regarded as the strongest that could be made, and that such works, defended by 20,000 men, would be impregnable as against my force, and not feeling very much encouraged by the information given me, I nevertheless replied to my informant that if that was all they had to oppose us we would not mind that. I have no doubt that some of my men, even after they were made prisoners, did what is called some "very tall talking" about my strength and purposes, and doubtless such boasting on their part contributed in no small degree to the state of bewilderment of my opponent in the subsequent campaign as to my strength and the success of my efforts to baffle him for so long a period.*[342]

So how many troops did Early really have at Silver Spring? We'll never definitively know.

NOTES

PREFACE

1. Silver Spring, without quotation marks, is used herein to denote the area. "Silver Spring," with quotation marks, is used to denote Francis Preston Blair's "Silver Spring" estate or mansion except in direct quotations when the context is clear.

CHAPTER 1

2. Judge, *Season of Fire*, 214.
3. *Hagerstown Herald of Freedom and Torch Light*, "The Result in Maryland," November 14, 1860, B2.
4. Leech, *Reveille in Washington*, 55.
5. *Evening Star*, "The Negro Act," November 8, 1860, 2.
6. *Hagerstown Herald of Freedom and Torch Light*, "The Result in Maryland"; Montgomery County 1860 Presidential Election Returns Transmittal Letter to the Governor, Maryland State Archives, MdHR # 40, 132-1658/1679; MSA S108-37; Location 02/50/01/022.

CHAPTER 2

7. Blair, "Annals of Silver Spring," 165.

8. Ibid., 163–66.

9. *Washington Post*, "General Lee Had the Opportunity to Command the United States Army in the Struggle Which Saved the Union," January 19, 1915, 11.

10. Maryland Historical Trust, Maryland Inventory of Historic Properties Form: Riggs-Thompson House. Survey No. M:36/8, section 8.2; "Petition of George W. Riggs, 27 May 1862," microfilm record from the National Archives, civilwardc.org/texts/petitions/cww.00478.html.

11. Nalewajk, *Woodside*, 16.

12. Furgurson, *Freedom Rising*, 12.

13. U.S. Bureau of the Census, Population of the 100 Largest Places, 1860, www.census.gov/population/www/documentation/twps0027/tab09.txt.

14. Furgurson, *Freedom Rising*, 13.

CHAPTER 3

15. Farquhar, *Historic Montgomery County*, 28–29.

16. McMaster and Hiebert, *Grateful Remembrance*, 170–71; Connery, *Civil War Northern Virginia 1861*, 120.

17. Personal communication to the author from Jerry McCoy, president of the Silver Spring Historical Society, citing Ancestry.com, November 18, 2012; Winkle, *Lincoln's Citadel*, 235.

18. *New York Times*, "News from Washington," November 29, 1861, 8; Pyne, *History of the First New Jersey Cavalry*, 22–23.

19. *Evening Star*, "Local News," September 19, 1862, 3.

20. *Montgomery County Sentinel*, September 26, 1862, 3.

21. Personal communications with the author from Dave Rathbun based on a search of census and other records.

22. Military records for John Marra, Company K, Twenty-second Massachusetts Infantry, National Archives; personal communications with the author from Dave Rathbun based on a search of census records.

23. Military records for William H. Rafferty, Company K, Twenty-second Massachusetts Infantry, National Archives; personal communications with the author from Dave Rathbun based on a search of census and other records.

24. Court-martial trial record of William H. Rafferty, National Archives, identifier 1814284, local identifier LL-88 (Records Group 153).

25. Ibid.; 1867 Maryland Slave Census, Maryland State Archives.

26. Personal communications with the author from Dave Rathbun based on a search of census and other records.

27. Court-martial trial record of William H. Rafferty, National Archives.

28. *Evening Star*, advertisements, November 15, 18, 21, 25 and 29, 1862, all on page 3.

29. Manakee, *Maryland in the Civil War*, 60.

30. *Evening Star*, public sale advertisement, November 14 and 26, 1862, both on page 3.

31. Laas, *Wartime Washington*, 209. This and all subsequently quoted letters from Elizabeth Blair Lee to her husband have been edited for clarity. Elizabeth Blair Lee frequently used uncommon abbreviations and eschewed most punctuation except dashes.

32. Ibid., 233.

33. *Evening Star*, "Spreading Themselves," June 29, 1863, 2.

34. Encyclopedia Virginia, www.encyclopediavirginia.org/ stuart_j_e_b_1833-1864#start_entry.

35. Leech, *Reveille in Washington*, 256.

CHAPTER 4

36. United States War Department, *Official Records*, ser. 1, vol. 40, part 2, 667. Subsequently cited as *Official Records*.

37. Vandiver, *Jubal's Raid*, 75.

38. Bernard, "Report on the Defenses of Washington," 110–11, quoting Early, *Memoir of the Last Year*.

39. Vandiver, *Jubal's Raid*, 92, 107; Middletown "Middle of What" Historical Marker, Middletown, Maryland.

40. Furgurson, *Freedom Rising*, 308.

41. *Evening Star*, "Affairs in Montgomery County, Md.," July 8, 1864, 4; *Evening Star*, "Set at Liberty," August 23, 1864, 2; *Daily National Republican*, "Local Affairs," August 24, 1864, second edition, 2; Nalewajk, *Woodside*, 16.

42. *Official Records*, ser. 1, vol. 37, part 2, 15.

43. Ibid., 60.

44. Ibid., 98; Leech, *Reveille in Washington*, 331–33.

45. *Evening Star*, "The Invasion of Maryland," July 14, 1864, 2.

46. Leepson, *Desperate Engagement*, 133–37.

47. Welles, *Diary of Gideon Welles*, 69–70.
48. Laas, *Wartime Washington*, 401–2, 411; Goodwin, *Team of Rivals*, 640; Welles, *Diary of Gideon Welles*, 69–70.
49. Welles, *Diary of Gideon Welles*, 70.
50. Leech, *Reveille in Washington*, 334.
51. Leepson, *Desperate Engagement*, 131; Mills, *Chesapeake Bay*, 246.
52. Leepson, *Desperate Engagement*, 121–32.
53. Ibid., 221.
54. "John W. Garrett, President, B&O Railroad," National Park Service, Monocacy National Battlefield, www.nps.gov/mono/historyculture/john_w_garrett.htm.
55. *Official Records*, ser. 1, vol. 37, part 2, 134.
56. Ibid., 155.
57. Ibid., ser. 1, vol. 40, part 3, 123.
58. Leepson, *Desperate Engagement*, 142–45.
59. Hyde, *Following the Greek Cross*, 221.
60. Miller, *Second Only to Grant*, 238–39.
61. Crew, *Centennial History*, 264.
62. Leepson, *Desperate Engagement*, 157–61.

CHAPTER 5

63. *Evening Star*, "Affairs in Montgomery County, MD," July 8, 1864, 4.
64. Duckett, "Prisoners of War," 316.
65. *Constitutional Union*, "The Situation and Excitement," July 11, 1864, 2.
66. Ibid.
67. Cox, "Defense of Washington," 144.
68. *Official Records*, ser. 1, vol. 37, part 1, 183.
69. Leepson, *Desperate Engagement*, 125.
70. Leech, *Reveille in Washington*, 334.
71. Leepson, *Desperate Engagement*, 139; Leech, *Reveille in Washington*, 336.
72. Brooks, *Washington in Lincoln's Time*, 175.
73. Furgurson, *Freedom Rising*, 319.
74. J.H. Johnston, "A Mansion's History of Insecurity," *Washington Post*, July 3, 2003, District Weekly, 9.
75. Welles, *Diary of Gideon Welles*, 71.
76. Ibid.
77. Leepson, *Desperate Engagement*, 138.

78. Ibid.
79. Ibid., 142.
80. Ibid., 141; *Evening Star*, "The Invasion," July 11, 1864, 1.
81. *Evening Star*, "The Invasion," July 11, 1864, 1.
82. Leech, *Reveille in Washington*, 337; Brooks, *Washington in Lincoln's Time*, 175.
83. James F. Fitts, "Grant, Halleck, and Wallace" (Letter to the Editor), *New York Times*, January 25, 1886, 5.
84. Brooks, *Washington in Lincoln's Time*, 173–74.
85. Leepson, *Desperate Engagement*, 140.
86. Ibid.

CHAPTER 6

87. Bernard, "A Report on the Defenses of Washington," 85.
88. Leepson, *Desperate Engagement*, 154.
89. Ibid., 151.
90. The name had been changed from the Invalid Corps to the Veteran Reserve Corps largely because the members of the corps hated the old name, which shared its initials, IC, with the terminology used by the army for worn-out horses, "Inspected and Condemned." Winkle, *Lincoln's Citadel*, 391–92.
91. Leepson, *Desperate Engagement*, 151–54.
92. CEHP Incorporated, *Historic Resources Study: The Civil War Defenses of Washington*, Part I, Chapter VII, www.cr.nps.gov/history/online_books/civilwar/hrs1-6.htm.

CHAPTER 7

93. Dunning, "Notes from a Diary," 310; Duckett, "Prisoners of War," 308.
94. *Evening Star*, "Further from the Fighting Near Rockville," July 11, 1864, 2.
95. Laas, *Wartime Washington*, 410.
96. *Official Records*, ser. 1, vol. 37, part 2, 415.
97. Ibid.
98. Early, *Autobiographical Sketch*, 389.
99. Roe, *Ninth New York Heavy Artillery*, 318–19.
100. Cox, "Defense of Washington," 145.
101. *Evening Star*, July 11, 1864, 2.

102. *New York Times*, "The Invasion," July 14, 1864, 1.

103. *Evening Star*, "The Invasion," July 11, 1864, 2.

104. Laas, *Wartime Washington*, 413–14.

105. *Evening Star*, "Interesting Particulars of the Rebel Invasion," July 15, 1864, 2; "Martenet and Bond's Map of Montgomery County, Maryland from Actual Surveys by S.J. Martenet & Assistants" (Baltimore, MD: Simon J. Martenet, 1865).

106. *Evening Star*, "Interesting Particulars of the Rebel Invasion," July 15, 1864, 2

107. *National Intelligencer*, "Conduct of the Invaders," July 16, 1864, 2.

108. *Official Records*, ser. 1, vol. 37, part 1, 415.

109. *New York Times*, "Review of the Rebel Raid," July 15, 1864, 1.

110. Ibid.

111. Ibid.

112. *Evening Star*, "The Invasion," July 11, 1864, 2; *Evening Star*, "The Invasion," July 12, 1864, 2.

113. Cooling and Owen, *Mr. Lincoln's Forts*, 156.

114. *New York Times*, "The Engagements Before Washington as Viewed by a Soldier," July 18, 1864.

115. Walker, *Vermont Brigade*, 28.

116. *Official Records*, ser. 1, vol. 37, part 1, 231.

117. Ibid.

118. *Evening Star*, July 11, 1864, 2.

119. Leepson, *Desperate Engagement*, 169.

120. Ibid., 168.

121. Ibid., 152; *Constitutional Union*, "Official," July 12, 1864, 2; Brooks, *Washington in Lincoln's Time*, 174.

122. Cox, "Defense of Washington," 141.

123. *New York Times*, "The Engagements Before Washington," July 18, 1864.

124. Chittenden, *Recollections of President Lincoln*, 409.

125. *Official Records*, ser. 1, vol. 37, part 1, 253.

126. Brooks, *Washington in Lincoln's Time*, 176.

127. *Evening Star*, "The Invasion," July 12, 1864, 2.

128. Ibid.; Crew, *Centennial History*, 273.

129. *Evening Star*, "The Invasion," July 12, 1864, 2; National Park Service, "The Civil War Defenses of Washington Historic Resources Study," www.cr.nps.gov/history/online_books/civilwar/hrs1-i.htm.

130. Leech, *Reveille in Washington*, 338.

131. Early, *Autobiographical Sketch*, 389.

132. Ibid., 390–91.

133. Ibid.

134. Ibid.

135. *New York Times*, "Review of the Rebel Raid," July 15, 1864, 1.

136. Cox, "Defense of Washington," 145.

137. Ibid., 147; *New York Times*, "Review of the Rebel Raid," July 15, 1864, 1.

138. Early, "Advance on Washington," 306.

139. Gordon, *Reminiscences of the Civil War*, 314.

140. Ibid., 314–15.

141. Bernard, "Report on the Defenses of Washington," 122 (quoting Jubal A. Early in *Southern Magazine*, June 1871).

142. Cooling, *Jubal Early's Raid*, 118.

143. [Hamblin], *Brevet Major-General Joseph Eldridge Hamblin*, 39.

144. Walker, *Vermont Brigade*, 28.

145. Leepson, *Desperate Engagement*, 169, 172; Judge, *Season of Fire*, 238.

146. Hyde, *Following the Greek Cross*, 222–23.

147. *New York Times*, "The Engagements Before Washington," July 18, 1864.

148. Worsham, *One of Jackson's Foot Cavalry*, 241–42.

149. *Evening Star*, "The Invasion," July 12, 1864, 2.

150. *National Intelligencer*, "The Rebel Wounded," July 15, 1864, 3.

151. *New York Times*, "The Raid on Washington—Gen. Jubal A. Early Again Tells His Story," August 6, 1881.

152. *Evening Star*, "The Invasion," July 12, 1864, 2.

153. *Official Records*, ser. 1, vol. 37, part 1, 242.

154. Ibid., 238.

155. Ibid.

156. Bradwell, "Early's March to Washington," 177.

157. Ibid.

CHAPTER 8

158. Bernard, "Report on the Defenses of Washington," 117–18 (quoting Early, *Memoir of the Last Year*).

159. *Evening Star*, "The Invasion," July 12, 1864, 2.

160. Welles, *Diary of Gideon Welles*, 72–73.

161. *National Intelligencer*, "Skirmishing Near Fort Stevens," July 13, 1864, 3.

162. Chittenden, *Recollections of President Lincoln*, 410.

CHAPTER 9

163. *Evening Star*, "The Invasion," July 12, 1864, 2.

164. *Official Records*, ser. 1, vol. 37, part 2, 234.

165. *Constitutional Union*, "Trip to Fort Stevens," July 12, 1864, 2.

166. *Official Records*, ser. 1, vol. 37, part 2, 234.

167. *Constitutional Union*, "The Excitement," July 13, 1864, 2; *Evening Star*, "Falls Church Occupied by the Rebels," July 12, 1864, 2; *National Intelligencer*, "Falls Church Occupied by Rebels," July 13, 1864, 3.

168. *New York Times*, "Review of the Rebel Raid," July 15, 1864, 1.

169. *Constitutional Union*, "Official," July 12, 1864, 2; *Evening Star*, "Yet Later," July 12, 1864, 2.

170. *New York Times*, "Review of the Rebel Raid," July 15, 1864, 1.

171. *New York Times*, "Rebel Shooting with the Long Bow," August 7, 1864, 4.

172. Bernard, "Report on the Defenses of Washington," 117–18 (quoting Early, *Memoir of the Last Year*).

173. Worsham, *One of Jackson's Foot Cavalry*, 242–43.

174. *Evening Star*, "Yet Later," July 12, 1864, 2.

175. *Constitutional Union*, "Trip to Fort Stevens," July 12, 1864, 2.

176. Ibid.; National Park Service, "The Civil War Defenses of Washington Historic Resources Study," www.cr.nps.gov/history/online_books/civilwar/hrs1-i.htm.

177. *Evening Star*, "The Invasion," July 12, 1864, 2.

178. *Official Records*, ser. 1, vol. 37, part 2, 223.

179. Welles, *Diary of Gideon Welles*, 74.

180. Ibid., 74–75.

181. Ibid., 75–76.

182. Nevin, "Fort Stevens," 37.

183. *Constitutional Union*, "Trip to Fort Stevens," July 12, 1864, 2; *Evening Star*, "Yet Later," July 12, 1864, 2.

184. *Official Records*, ser. 1, vol. 37, part 2, 265.

185. *Evening Star*, "Important Documents," July 16, 1864, 2.

186. Ibid.

187. Chittenden, *Recollections of President Lincoln*, 412.

188. *Evening Star*, "The Invasion," July 13, 1864, 2.

189. *Evening Star*, "Official," July 13, 1864, 2.

190. *Constitutional Union*, "Trip to Fort Stevens," July 12, 1864, 2.

191. Ibid.

192. *Evening Star*, "The Invasion," July 13, 1864, 2.

193. Cooling and Owen, *Mr. Lincoln's Forts*, 159–61.

194. Hyde, *Following the Greek Cross*, 223.

195. Nevin, "Fort Stevens," 44.

196. *New York Times*, "President Lincoln at Fort Stevens," February 10, 1907, 15.

197. Ibid.

198. *New York Times*, "President Lincoln Hit by a Confederate Bullet," January 13, 1907.

199. *Evening Star*, "The Invasion," July 13, 1864, 2.

200. *Constitutional Union*, "The Fight Last Night," July 13, 1864, 2.

201. *Evening Star*, "The Invasion," July 13, 1864, 2.

202. *National Intelligencer*, "Retreat of the Enemy," July 14, 1864, 3.

203. Leepson, *Desperate Engagement*, 206.

204. Chittenden, *Recollections of President Lincoln*, 418–19.

205. Ibid., 419.

206. Ibid., 419–20.

207. Ibid., 420.

208. *Official Records*, ser. 1, vol. 37, part 1, 242.

209. *Evening Star*, "Interesting Particulars on the Rebel Invasion," July 15, 1864, 2.

210. *National Intelligencer*, "Conduct of the Invaders," July 16, 1864, 2.

211. Bradwell, "Early's March to Washington," 177.

212. *National Republican*, "Gen. Jubal A. Early Tells His Story," August 4, 1881, 1.

213. Ibid.

214. Leeke, *A Hundred Days to Richmond*, 135.

215. Early, *Memoir of the Last Year*, 59.

216. Judge, *Season of Fire*, 255.

217. Ibid.

CHAPTER 10

218. *Official Records*, ser. 1, vol. 37, part 1, 253.

219. Duckett, "Prisoners of War," 308.

220. *Official Records*, ser. 1, vol. 37, part 1, 253.

221. Ibid., 232.

222. Ibid., 232–33.

223. Ibid., part 2, 263.

224. *Evening Star*, "The Invasion," July 13, 1864, 2.

225. *Official Records*, ser. 1, vol. 37, part 2, 260.

226. Judge, *Season of Fire*, 258.
227. *Official Records*, ser. 1, vol. 37, part 2, 415.
228. Ibid., 267.
229. *Evening Star*, "The Invasion," July 13, 1864, 2; *Evening Star*, "Late and Important," July 13, 1864, 2; *Evening Star*, "The Rebel Rear Guard Crossing the River at Poolsville," July 14, 1864, 2.
230. *Evening Star*, "A Brave Cavalryman," July 16, 1864, 2.
231. Goodwin, *Team of Rivals*, 644.
232. *Evening Star*, "Confederate Dead—Removal of Remains Today," December 11, 1874, 4; Getty, *To Light the Way*, 9.
233. *Official Records*, ser. 1, vol. 37, part 2, 385–86.
234. Ibid., 308.
235. Ibid., part 1, 256.
236. Ibid., 260.
237. Roe, *Ninth New York Heavy Artillery*, 159.
238. *Evening Star*, "Further of the Rebel Retreat," July 13, 1864, 2.
239. *Official Records*, ser. 1, vol. 37, part 2, 262–63.
240. Laas, *Wartime Washington*, 402–3.
241. Ibid., 403.
242. *Constitutional Union*, "The Excitement," July 13, 1864, 2.
243. Foreman, *World on Fire*, 639.
244. *National Intelligencer*, "The City Militia and Volunteers," July 14, 1864, 3.
245. *Official Records*, ser. 1, vol. 37, part 2, 384–85.
246. Roe, *Ninth New York Heavy Artillery*, 158.
247. Laas, *Wartime Washington*, 416.
248. Ibid., 420.

CHAPTER 11

249. Judge, *Season of Fire*, 249, quoting Chittenden.
250. *Official Records*, ser. 1, vol. 37, part 2, 268.
251. *Evening Star*, "The Rebel Inversion [*sic*]," July 14, 1864, 2.
252. Judge, *Season of Fire*, 260.
253. Cooling, *Jubal Early's Raid*, 153.
254. Laas, *Wartime Washington*, 404–5. According to Walker, *Vermont Brigade*, 32: "A carte-de-visite of some Virginia beauty was found [in the "Silver Spring" mansion] in the side of a mirror, on the back of which had

been pencilled the following: 'Taken from a pilferer for old acquaintance sake with Miss Emma Mason, and left at 11 p.m. here by a Rebel officer who once knew her and remained behind to prevent this house from being burned by stragglers as was the neighboring one, 11 p.m., and no light, July 12, 1864.'" Walker went on to say: "The photograph was left where found, but it may never have reached the family, as credit of the preservation of the house was given to General Breckinridge by the newspapers. The above shows how much he deserved it. He had not then become the 'extinct volcano' he has recently dubbed himself." We now know from Elizabeth Lee's letters that the note did, indeed, reach the family.

255. Laas, *Wartime Washington*, 404–5.
256. Welles, *Diary of Gideon Welles*, 80–81.
257. Laas, *Wartime Washington*, 407 (note 1).
258. Ibid., 407.
259. Ibid., 405.
260. Ibid., 128 (note 5).
261. Ibid., 411.
262. Ibid., 412.
263. Ibid.
264. Ibid., 416.
265. Ibid., 405 (note 2).
266. Ibid., 416.
267. Ibid., 417.
268. *Evening Star*, classified advertisement, October 28, 1863, 3.
269. *National Republican*, "Gen. Jubal A. Early Tells His Story," August 4, 1881, 1.
270. Leech, *Reveille in Washington*, 345.
271. Laas, *Wartime Washington*, 412 (note 1).
272. Ibid., 405 (note 2).
273. Judge, *Season of Fire*, 260.
274. Getty, *To Light the Way*, 91.
275. *Official Records*, ser. 1, vol. 37, part 2, 415–16.
276. Laas, *Wartime Washington*, 404–5.
277. *New York Times*, "Another Dispatch," July 22, 1864, 1.
278. Ibid.
279. Ibid.
280. *Instructions for the Government of Armies of the United States in the Field, Prepared by Francis Lieber, LL.D., Originally Issued as General Orders No. 100, Adjutant General's Office, 1863* (Washington, D.C.: Government Printing Office, 1898).

281. *Constitutional Union*, "The Latest," July 13, 1864, 2; *New York Times*, "Review of the Rebel Raid," July 15, 1864, 1.

282. *Evening Star*, "Interesting Particulars of the Rebel Invasion," July 15, 1864, 2.

283. *Evening Star*, "The Rebel Inversion [*sic*]," July 14, 1864, 2.

284. *Evening Star*, "From Up the River," July 16, 1864, 2.

285. Laas, *Wartime Washington*, 421.

286. Montgomery County Land Records, Liber EBP 1, folio 281, Maryland State Archives.

287. Laas, *Wartime Washington*, 422.

288. *National Intelligencer*, "Conduct of the Invaders," July 16, 1864, 2, quoting the *Chronicle*.

289. *New York Times*, "Review of the Rebel Raid," July 15, 1864, 1; Jane Ohlmacher of the Bonifant family conversation with Marilyn Slatick; e-mail to the author, November 30, 2009.

290. Brooks, *Washington in Lincoln's Time*, 178–79.

291. Getty, *To Light the Way*, 12.

292. Nalewajk, *Woodside*, 20.

293. Ibid., 20–21.

294. *Official Records*, ser. 1, vol. 37, part 2, 415.

295. Personal communications to the author from Loetta Vann, October 17, 2009, and Betty Kramer, October 28, 2013; *Washington Post*, real estate advertisement, August 27, 1966, D7.

296. *Evening Star*, "Interesting Particulars of the Rebel Invasion," July 15, 1864, 2.

297. Ibid.

298. Laas, *Wartime Washington*, 416.

299. Dana, *Recollections of the Civil War*, 231–32.

300. Goodwin, *Team of Rivals*, 519, 525–26.

301. Lincoln, *Collected Works of Abraham Lincoln*, 440–41.

302. Brooks, *Abraham Lincoln*, 438.

303. Blair, "Annals of Silver Spring," 177–78.

304. Goodwin, *Team of Rivals*, 645.

305. Ibid., 658–59.

306. Laas, *Wartime Washington*, 420.

307. Foreman, *World on Fire*, 640.

308. Brooks, *Washington in Lincoln's Time*, 177.

309. Walston, "Three Days in July."

310. *Official Records*, ser. 1, vol. 47, part 3, 577.

311. *Evening Star*, "Strawberry Party," May 31, 1865, 3.

CHAPTER 12

312. Harris, "Hampton Roads Peace Conference."

313. Ibid.

314. Ibid.

315. Ibid.

316. Dickinson, "Confederate Peace Resolutions"; "The Civil War's Last Great Peace Effort," www.civilwarhome.com/peaceconference.htm.

317. Harris, "Hampton Roads Peace Conference."

CHAPTER 13

318. *Evening Star*, "Confederate Dead—Removal of Remains To-Day," December 11, 1874, 4.

319. Personal communication to the author from David Rathbun citing the Virginia Regimental History Series, www.civilwardata.com, November 4, 2013.

320. *Evening Star*, "Confederate Dead—Removal of Remains To-Day," December 11, 1874, 4.

321. Getty, *To Light the Way*, 9.

322. Crew, *Centennial History*, 270.

323. *Evening Star*, "Confederate Dead—Removal of Remains To-Day," December 11, 1874, 4.

324. Getty, *To Light the Way*, 11–12.

325. Ibid.

326. Ibid., 15–16.

327. *Evening Star*, "Rockville," November 9, 1896, 10.

328. *Montgomery County Sentinel*, November 20, 1896; *Evening Star*, "Confederate Monument," November 14, 1896, 1; *Washington Post*, "Fell in Early's Raid," November 15, 1896, 8.

329. *Evening Star*, "Confederate Monument," November 14, 1896, 1.

330. Personal communication to the author from David Rathbun, November 3, 2013.

APPENDIX

331. *Evening Star*, "The Rebel Force in Front of Us—Its Strength and Purpose," July 11, 1864, 2

332. Ibid.

333. *National Intelligencer*, "The Late Siege of Washington," July 14, 1864, 3.

334. Worsham, *One of Jackson's Foot Cavalry*, 241.

335. *Official Records*, ser. 1, vol. 37, part 2, 330.

336. Dunning, "Notes from a Diary," 310.

337. *Official Records*, ser. 1, vol. 37, part 1, 233.

338. Chittenden, *Recollections of President Lincoln*, 407.

339. *Official Records*, ser. 1, vol. 37, part 2, 415–16.

340. Ibid., 414.

341. *National Republican*, "Gen. Jubal A. Early Tells His Story of the Raid on Washington in July 1864," August 4, 1881, 1.

342. Ibid.

BIBLIOGRAPHY

Bernard, John Gross. "A Report on the Defenses of Washington to the Chief of Engineers, U.S. Army by Brevet Major General John Gross Barnard, Colonel, Corps of Engineers, U.S. Army." In *Professional Papers of the Corps of Engineers, U.S. Army* 20. Washington, D.C.: Government Printing Office, 1871.

Blair, Gist. "Annals of Silver Spring." *Records of the Columbia Historical Society* 21 (1918).

Bradwell, I.G. "Early's March to Washington in 1864." *Confederate Veteran* (May 1920).

Brooks, Noah. *Abraham Lincoln.* New York: G.P. Putnam's Sons, 1888.

———. *Washington in Lincoln's Time.* New York: Century Company, 1895.

Chittenden, L.E. *Recollections of President Lincoln and His Administration.* New York: Harper & Brothers, 1891.

Connery, William S. *Civil War Northern Virginia 1861.* Charleston, SC: The History Press, 2011.

Cooling, Benjamin Franklin. *Jubal Early's Raid on Washington 1864.* Baltimore, MD: Nautical & Aviation Publishing Company of America, 1989.

Cooling, Benjamin Franklin, and Walton H. Owen. *Mr. Lincoln's Forts: A Guide to the Civil War Defenses of Washington.* Shippensburg, PA: White Mane Publishing Company, 1988.

Cox, William V. "The Defense of Washington—General Early's Advance on the Capital and the Battle of Fort Stevens, July 11 and 12, 1864." *Records of the Columbia Historical Society* 4 (1901).

Crew, Harvey W., ed. *Centennial History of the City of Washington, D.C.* Dayton, OH: United Brethren Publishing House, 1892.

Dana, Charles Anderson. *Recollections of the Civil War: With the Leaders at Washington and in the Field in the Sixties.* New York: D. Appleton and Company, 1913.

Dickinson, Jack L. "The Confederate Peace Resolutions and Negotiations of 1864–1865." November 2010. www.marshall.edu/library/speccoll/virtual_ museum/hampton_roads/pdf/ConfederatePeaceResolutions-1.pdf.

Duckett, W.G. "Prisoners of War: My Capture and Escape." In *The Ninth New York Heavy Artillery*, by Alfred Seeyle Roe. Worcester, MA: self-published, 1899.

Dunning, E.P. "Notes from a Diary Kept in Danville Prison." In *The Ninth New York Heavy Artillery*, by Alfred Seeyle Roe. Worcester, MA: self-published, 1899.

Early, Jubal A. "The Advance on Washington in 1864." *Southern Historical Society Papers* 9, nos. 7 and 8 (July and August 1881).

———. *Autobiographical Sketch and Narrative of the War Between the States.* Philadelphia: J.B. Lippincott Company, 1912.

———. *A Memoir of the Last Year of the War for Independence, in the Confederate States of America.* Lynchburg, VA: Charles W. Button, 1867.

Farquhar, Roger Brooke. *Historic Montgomery County, Maryland.* Baltimore, MD: Monumental Printing Company, 1952.

Foreman, Amanda. *A World on Fire.* New York: Random House, 2010.

Furgurson, Ernest B. *Freedom Rising: Washington in the Civil War.* New York: Alfred A. Knopf, 2004.

Getty, Mildred Newbold. *To Light the Way: A History of Grace Episcopal Church.* Silver Spring, MD: Grace Episcopal Church, 1965.

Goodwin, Doris Kearns. *Team of Rivals.* New York: Simon and Schuster, 2005.

Gordon, John G. *Reminiscences of the Civil War.* New York: Charles Scribner's Sons, 1904.

[Hamblin, Deborah]. *Brevet Major-General Joseph Eldridge Hamblin, 1861–65.* Boston: privately printed, 1902.

Harris, William C. "The Hampton Roads Peace Conference: A Final Test of Lincoln's Presidential Leadership." *Journal of the Abraham Lincoln Association* 21, no. 1 (Winter 2000). hdl.handle.net/2027/spo.2629860.0021.104.

Hyde, Thomas W. *Following the Greek Cross or Memories of the Sixth Army Corps.* Boston: Houghton Mifflin and Company, 1894.

Judge, Joseph. *Season of Fire: The Confederate Strike on Washington.* Berryville, VA: Rockbridge Publishing Company, 1994.

Laas, Virginia, ed. *Wartime Washington: The Civil War Letters of Elizabeth Blair Lee.* Urbana: University of Illinois Press, 1999.

Leech, Margaret. *Reveille in Washington 1860–1865*. New York: Harper & Brothers, 1941.

Leeke, Jim, ed. *A Hundred Days to Richmond: Ohio's "Hundred Days" Men in the Civil War*. Bloomington: Indiana University Press, 1999.

Leepson, Marc. *Desperate Engagement*. New York: Thomas Dunne Books, 2007.

Lincoln, Abraham. Edited by Roy P. Basler. *Collected Works of Abraham Lincoln*. Vol. 7. New Brunswick, NJ: Rutgers University Press, 1953.

Manakee, Harold R. *Maryland in the Civil War*. Baltimore: Maryland State Historical Society, 1961.

McMaster, Richard K., and Ray Eldon Hiebert. *A Grateful Remembrance: The Story of Montgomery County, Maryland*. Rockville, MD: Montgomery County Government and Montgomery County Historical Society, 1976.

Miller, David W. *Second Only to Grant: Quartermaster General Montgomery C. Meigs*. Shippensburg, PA: White Mane Books, 2000.

Mills, Eric. *Chesapeake Bay in the Civil War*. Centerville, MD: Tidewater Publishers, 1996.

Nalewajk, Joyce E. *Woodside: The Early Years*. Preliminary Edition. Silver Spring, MD: Woodside Civic Association, 1991.

Nevin, D.R.B. "Fort Stevens." *The United Service* 2 (July 1889). New Series.

Pyne, Henry R. *The History of the First New Jersey Cavalry*. Trenton, NJ: JA Beecher, Publisher, 1871.

Roe, Alfred Seelye. *The Ninth New York Heavy Artillery*. Worcester, MA: self-published, 1899.

United States War Department. *The War of the Rebellion: A Compilation of the Official Records of the Union and Confederate Armies*. Series I, vols. 37 and 40. Washington, D.C.: Government Printing Office, 1891, 1892.

Vandiver, Frank E. *Jubal's Raid: General Early's Famous Attack on Washington in 1864*. Lincoln: University of Nebraska Press, 1992.

Walker, Aldace F. *The Vermont Brigade in the Shenandoah Valley, 1864*. Burlington, VT: Free Press Association, 1896.

Walston, Mark. "Three Days in July." *Bethesda Magazine* (November 2009). www.bethesdamagazine.com/Bethesda-Magazine/November-December-2009/Three-Days-in-July.

Welles, Gideon. *Diary of Gideon Welles*. Vol. 2. Boston: Houghton Mifflin Company, 1911.

Winkle, Kenneth J. *Lincoln's Citadel*. New York: W.W. Norton & Company, 2013.

Worsham, John. H. *One of Jackson's Foot Cavalry*. New York: Neal Publishing Company, 1912.

INDEX

INDEX

INDEX

About the Author

R obert E. Oshel, PhD, has written a number of local history publications concerning the Silver Spring area, including a history of the Silver Spring library, a historic and architectural walking tour of the Woodside Park neighborhood and the book *Home Sites of Distinction: The History of Woodside Park.* He writes a monthly history column for the *Woodside Park Voice.* His work has also appeared in the *Montgomery County Story,* a publication of the Montgomery County Historical Society. He has lectured on local history at events sponsored by the National Building Museum, the Maryland–National Capital Park and Planning Commission, the Latrobe Chapter of the Society of Architectural Historians and the Montgomery County Historical Society.

At his retirement in September 2008, Dr. Oshel was associate director for research and disputes of the National Practitioner Data Bank, U.S. Department of Health and Human Services. In connection with this position, Dr. Oshel also had an appointment as adjunct assistant professor of preventive medicine/biometrics at the Uniformed Services University of the Health Sciences, F. Edward Hebert School of Medicine. He is the author of numerous articles concerning the National Practitioner Data Bank, medical malpractice, medical discipline and related issues published in the *Bulletin of the American College of Surgeons, American Academy of Pediatrics News, American*

Association of Nurse Anesthetists Journal, Quality Review in Anesthesia, Texas Medicine, Legal Medicine, Public Health Reports and *JAMA*.

Dr. Oshel lives with his wife, Kay, in the Woodside Park neighborhood of Silver Spring, Maryland.